POLICE COMMUNITY SUPPORT OFFICERS

CLARENDON STUDIES IN CRIMINOLOGY

Published under the auspices of the Institute of Criminology, University of Cambridge; the Mannheim Centre, London School of Economics; and the Centre for Criminology, University of Oxford.

RECENT TITLES IN THIS SERIES:

Last Chance for Life: Clemency in Southeast Asian Death Penalty Cases
Pascoe

Police Unlimited: Policing, Migrants, and the Values of Bureaucracy
Mutsaers

Personalizing the State: An Anthropology of Law, Politics, and Welfare in Austerity Britain
Koch

Common Enemies: Crime, Policy, and Politics in Australia-Indonesia Relations
McKenzie

Embodying Punishment: Emotions, Identities, and Lived Experiences in Women's Prisons
Chamberlen

Professionalizing the Police: The Unfulfilled Promise of Police Training
Fielding

Getting Out: Early Release in England and Wales, 1960–1995
Guiney

Sentencing Policy and Social Justice
Henham

Police Community Support Officers

Cultures and Identities within Pluralized Policing

MEGAN O'NEILL

OXFORD
UNIVERSITY PRESS

OXFORD
UNIVERSITY PRESS

Great Clarendon Street, Oxford, OX2 6DP,
United Kingdom

Oxford University Press is a department of the University of Oxford.
It furthers the University's objective of excellence in research, scholarship,
and education by publishing worldwide. Oxford is a registered trade mark of
Oxford University Press in the UK and in certain other countries

First Edition published in 2019

Published in the United States of America by Oxford University Press
198 Madison Avenue, New York, NY 10016, United States of America

British Library Cataloguing in Publication Data
Data available

Library of Congress Control Number: 2018967780

ISBN 978–0–19–880367–6

For Sophie, fierce and strong

General Editors' Introduction

The *Clarendon Studies in Criminology* series aims to provide a forum for outstanding theoretical and empirical work in all aspects of criminology and criminal justice, broadly understood. The Editors welcome submissions from established scholars, as well as excellent PhD work. The Series was inaugurated in 1994, with Roger Hood as its first General Editor, following discussions between Oxford University Press and Oxford's Centre for Criminological Research. It is edited under the auspices of three centres: the Institute of Criminology at the University of Cambridge, the Mannheim Centre for Criminology at the London School of Economics, and the Centre for Criminological Research at the University of Oxford. Each supplies members of the Editorial Board and, in turn, the Series Editor or Editors.

British policing is constantly required to address new challenges, whether this be a rise in knife crime or new crimes emerging with ever-changing technology. New challenges require consideration of resources, with successive police chiefs arguing that the job cannot be done, or done well, without an increase in resources, and particularly person-power. The Police Reform Act 2002 introduced the role of the Police Community Support Officer (PCSO) as an additional actor in the policing landscape, with every intention of making the police more visible, though PCSOs do not have the same powers or authority as the police. This book captures the changing nature of British policing extremely well, focusing on the pluralization and civilianization of the police, with ever-widening roles and reach, but also the vulnerability of PCSOs in the policing structure, and in a context of austerity. PCSOs work alongside police officers, and from the same police stations, so are thus subject to many of the same occupational culture, demands and expectations.

This book focuses on three main themes: public sector pluralization, community policing, and the police occupational culture. The aim is to further our understanding of ways in which PCSOs have become embedded within police operations and occupational culture, a task in which the author succeeds very well. There is previous research on PCSOs and the wider community, but very little on the interaction of PCSOs and police officers working from the same police stations. The author cleverly utilizes Goffman's notion of 'performance' in order to describe how PCSOs attempt to persuade police colleagues (and the public) of their 'authority' even if they do not have the powers that police officers have. The author's focus on how PCSOs learn their craft and on the interaction of PCSOs and police officers is fascinating, drawing on a six-month ethnographic study in six Neighbourhood Policing Teams across two police forces in England. We learn what motivates PCSOs, with altruism featuring alongside more instrumental factors; we also learn about some of the limitations and frustrations of the training they receive. And we also learn about ways in which the structure in which PCSOs operate serves to undermine their roles and purpose.

This work will undoubtedly appeal to academic researchers with an interest in both policing in general and, in particular, in the civilianization of the police as a public service. As Editors, we commend this book for making a significant contribution to the field of criminology and to our understanding of the complexities policing in the early 21st century. The book shines a thoughtful and thought-provoking spotlight on an important element of contemporary policing. We warmly welcome *Police Community Support Officers: Cultures and Identities within Pluralized Policing* to the *Clarendon Studies in Criminology* series.

Loraine Gelsthorpe and Kyle Treiber
Institute of Criminology,
University of Cambridge
March, 2019

Preface

The British policing landscape is an ever-changing one. Over the years police forces have been created and merged, technology has become an ever more central feature of the role, new governments bring in new policies and funding structures, and the legislation which officers are to enforce is constantly being re-written. A significant addition to this ever-changing landscape in England and Wales came in 2002 with the Police Reform Act. This introduced the role of Police Community Support Officer (PCSO) to public policing: support staff with a limited rage of powers who are intended to provide the visible policing presence that the public seemed to be demanding but which police officers were struggling to achieve. While the merits (or otherwise) of this role have been and are continuing to be debated, what is beyond contention is that the arrival of an additional actor in the public policing arena has had implications beyond the size and the nature of the workload of their fellow community police officers. Any new role within an occupation will affect the structure and the culture of that occupation, and none more so than in policing. It is these three interrelated themes—public sector pluralization, community policing, and the occupational culture in policing—which this book explores, through the lens of the actors at the centre of this storm, the PCSOs.

Research and scholarship on policing extends back several decades and across many countries. The cannon of literature has been shaped by many social and political events over the past 70 years. The policing arena which was studied by those first researchers in the 1950s and 1960s is in some respects unrecognizable from the one researchers encounter today. The number of women and minority ethnic officers has significantly increased; police collaboration with outside agencies is now taken as read rather than avoided; and increasing numbers of officers are educated to degree level. The focus and the goals of policing research has likewise changed and reoriented itself. For example, the call for 'evidence-based' policing is growing, as is the research to supply it, such as through experimental and quasi-experimental research design. However, one constant across these years and social and political fluctuations is an interest in the occupational culture of policing. While there is a significant amount of debate as to what the police occupational culture is and if it even exists at all in any meaningful way, it continues to fascinate and excite researchers of policing, myself included. This book is grounded in these debates, and it offers in its final section a revised vision of police culture, one which takes into account the undeniably pluralized policing field in which police officers now operate, especially in the context of community policing.

It is important at this point to acknowledge that the main subject of this book, the PCSO, is not, in fact, a police officer. As members of support staff, they do not have the same range of powers and experiences as police officers nor do they face the same extremes in terms of stress and trauma. PCSOs do not work overnight shifts; they cannot use force unless in self-defence; they do not have the power of arrest beyond that of any citizen; and they cannot attend high-priority calls such as sudden deaths or crimes in progress. That being said, as members of public police forces who dress in a similar uniform to and who often work alongside community police officers, PCSOs are exposed to the demands, expectations, and eccentricities of the public in ways complementary to that of police officers. Perhaps even more importantly in terms of occupational culture, PCSOs work within the same police forces and police stations as officers and are exposed to the same rank structure and informal methods of working and socializing as police constables are. While PCSOs are not the same as police officers, they draw their occupational experiences from a similar framework. It is thus valid to draw upon and situate this book within the existing academic literature on policing.

It is the task of Chapter 1 to do just that, to reflect upon the existing literature of the three main themes of the book: public sector pluralization, community policing, and the police occupational culture. They form the central context into which PCSOs arrived. Each of these informs and—as will be demonstrated during the course of the book—is informed by the role and experiences of PCSOs. First, the chapter will consider how the majority of the literature on pluralization examines issues related in some way to the private sector, rather than the effects of an increasingly pluralized public sector. Next, Chapter 1 turns to a discussion of community policing, which is the main area of police work in which PCSOs are located. Its traditionally low status in policing compounds the difficulties PCSOs have in gaining acceptance internally. Finally, the chapter explores the key areas of police culture research which have the most relevance for a discussion of PCSOs: bonding and alienation, storytelling, 'soft' policing, action orientation, and gender and ethnicity. Storytelling, in particular, will be explored again in the latter chapters of the book for its importance in the process of developing police occupational culture, as revealed by this examination of a pluralized public policing.

Chapter 2 presents the methods and structure of the research on pluralized public policing, a 6-month ethnographic study of PCSOs in England, the theoretical framework used to analyse it. The research examined in this book is a multisite ethnography, conducted in six neighbourhood policing teams (NPTs) across two police forces in England (three teams in each force). Each team was observed for a month, and several interviews of PCSOs and their police officer colleagues were conducted. This chapter provides descriptions of the research methods and of each NPT to give a context to the observations and analysis which follow in subsequent chapters. The second half of the chapter describes the dramaturgic metaphor used by Goffman in his text *The Presentation of Self in Everyday Life* (1959), and how it applies in the case of PCSOs. Dramaturgy is a useful tool for examining face-to-face interaction observed during ethnographic research, and it is employed in subsequent chapters, to analyse this level of interaction. Processes and decisions taken at a more macro-level also have bearing on the experiences of PCSOs (as we will see in Chapter 4), so while dramaturgy is less applicable here, the micro and macro levels inform each other and as such, will be brought back together in Part III.

The purpose of Chapter 3 is to explore what exactly PCSOs do in their work, as well as the skills seen as essential for these tasks. It begins with a description of a 'typical' day for PCSOs in terms of the patterns and rhythms which structure it. It then examines the types of policing work PCSOs perform, which includes enforcement-type activities, community engagement work, administration, and response to emergency situations. The chapter concludes with an analysis of the skills seen as most valuable for PCSOs to have: good communication and the development of local knowledge. What this chapter in effect presents is the ideal *definition of the situation* (Goffman 1959) for PCSOs. This is the performance which PCSOs try to portray in their encounters with police officers and members of the public. The next two chapters explore how this is challenged at an institutional level (Chapter 4) and in face-to-face encounters (Chapter 5).

Chapter 4 commences with an examination of what motivated the participants to apply to be a PCSO. A variety of push and pull factors are identified, some of which are instrumental in their orientation, whereas others are more altruistic or ideological. A discussion of the length and content of initial PCSO training is then presented, which starts to illustrate the ways in which the police organization has failed to adequately equip these staff for their role. The chapter concludes with a consideration of the ongoing training offered to PCSOs and the 'on the job' training in the field which they experience. All of these aspects of organizational socialization suggest that there is much less consideration given to the PCSO training period than there is for that of police officers, even taking account of their restricted role. This makes it difficult for the new recruits to learn the *definition of situation* they are meant to perform for others in their work, and it argues that PCSOs are in effect *institutionally undermined* by the very organization which employs them.

This process of institutional undermining provides the background context for personal interaction between PCSOs and their police officer colleagues, as explored next in Chapter 5. This chapter uses a dramaturgic analysis (Goffman 1959) to assess their interactions under the themes of performances, teamwork, and regions. PCSOs are under pressure regularly to prove their worth to police officers through a convincing presentation of self. However, as the chapter reveals, the extent to which PCSOs are integrated into the NPT will determine how these performances are enacted and how readily the definition of the situation which they present is accepted. It will be argued that PCSOs and police officers perform as two separate performance teams in either a *complementary* or *competitive* arrangement within each NPT.

Chapter 6 brings together the macro-level analysis of Chapter 4 and the micro-level analysis of Chapter 5 within the police culture framework proposed by Chan (1997), to assess the occupational culture of PCSOs. A novel focus on storytelling is used to highlight how occupational culture is developed and enacted, which reveals significant variation between the cultural processes of PCSOs and PCs. It also reveals that the methods PCSOs use to cope with institutional undermining vary depending on whether their performance teams are in complementary or competitive relationships with PC teams. The different processes of occupational culture used by PCs and PCSOs can at times result in similar cultural artefacts (Schein 1990), but this does not mean that the culture of the two groups is itself the same. This analysis of police occupational culture represents a departure from exiting scholarship.

The final chapter, Chapter 7, explores the book's analysis in light of more recent developments in the field of policing in England and Wales, and it reflects on how the cultural analysis presented here will have relevance for policing groups in other countries. In the time since the fieldwork was conducted, national changes to policy and legislation in policing have meant that the institutional undermining of PCSOs has been enhanced. This is likely to have significant implications for PCSOs' cultural responses, in both competitive and complementary community policing team configurations. Community policing is itself a pluralized policing method. While police auxiliary staff, such as PCSOs, are not in place in most police forces globally, community policing and other pluralized policing arrangements frequently feature. Therefore, the enhanced police culture framework developed in this text, which reflects contemporary conditions of pluralized policing in a way not previously attempted, will have salience in contexts far beyond the case of PCSOs in northern England. The importance of considering occupational culture in pluralized policing for any context is therefore highlighted because of the role it plays in the nature and outcome of these complex relationships.

Acknowledgements

This book as has been a labour of love for a number of years, and that kind of dedication and stamina would not have been possible without the support, encouragement, and patience of many people. Firstly, I would like to thank Peter Neyroud for giving me a good kick in the bum (metaphorically speaking) to get going on this writing project and for assisting with the initial contact with the editorial board at the Clarendon Series. To the editors at Oxford University Press, Peter Daniell, Amy Baker, and Lucy Alexander, I would like to extend my sincere thanks for all you have done to support me in this work and for your unfailing tolerance of my inability to accurately judge the time it takes for me to get thoughts on paper. I would also like to thank the Clarendon Series editorial board for considering this work in your series for allowing me the time needed to get the proposal into the best shape possible.

I have been blessed with many lovely and supportive colleagues across two universities over the years this book has developed, and to them I say a most sincere thank you. From Salford University, I am grateful for the support of Greg Smith (who read previous versions of material in these chapters and who is in general my go-to Goffman guru), Karl Dayson, Chris Birkbeck, and the rest of the Criminology group who supported me in a variety of ways to undertake the project on which this book is based. From the University of Dundee, I am grateful for the support of Mark Cutler, Beverley Searle, and Nick Fyfe for their encouragement and enthusiasm, and importantly, for the gift of time to work on the text. For my Geography colleagues who stepped in cover my absence from some of my duties during these periods, and for therapeutic coffee mornings, I am very grateful. Thank you.

Other scholars and friends have also provided me with invaluable guidance and support in the course of writing of this book and so deserve mention here. Many thanks to Jonathan Mendel and Karen Bullock for reading previous versions of text which appears here. Sincere thanks are also due to Daniel McCarthy and Anna Souhami for taking the time to read and comment on draft chapters (twice in Anna's case!). Your insights have made this a better book. I would like to thank Bethan Loftus for her unwavering encouragement in my endeavours, and especially for her guidance in the early stages of developing this text. Peter Manning has been a mentor for me throughout my career, and his influence is clearly evident in this project. Thank you for showing me that I am allowed to be the kind of policing scholar I want to be. Finally, I would like to thank Matt Bacon for mentioning me in his acknowledgements section, and Ian Thomson for being so subtle in his hints about wanting to be named in a 'proper' book. (And they might have had some supportive things to say along the way, too. Possibly.)

As ever with research of this kind, nothing would have been achieved without the participation of the many PCSOs and police officers, their supervisors, and members of the communities in which I conducted my fieldwork. Thank you so very much for sharing with me your insights, your time and the many cups of tea (and, on one occasion when I was particularly ill-prepared, your lunch) which helped to see me through many cold and damp shifts. There would be no book if it was not for you and your willingness to show me your working world. I am so very grateful. Particular thanks go to Hannah Crosby and Katie Teal for discussing current PCSO practice and policy with me to ensure that the text was up to date.

And finally, to my family: Boab, Aidan, and Sophie. You are my compass and my strength. I am who I am today because of you. Thank you.

* * *

The project on which this text is based was funded by the Leverhulme Trust Research Fellowship [grant number RF-2012-332].

Permissions to use extracts from two previously published articles are as follows:

This book is derived, in part, by an article published in *Policing and Society* on 25 March 2015 available online: https://www.tandfonline.com/doi/full/10.1080/10439463.2015.1020805. The full citation is: O'Neill, M. (2017/2015) 'Police community support officers in England: a dramaturgical analysis', *Policing and Society: An International Journal of Research and Policy*, 27 (1): 21–39.

O'Neill, M. (2014) 'The case for the acceptable "other": the impact of partnerships, PCSOs and Neighbourhood Policing on diversity in policing', *Policing: A Journal of Policy and Practice*: 9 (1): 77–88. By permission of Oxford University Press.

Table of Contents

PART I

Context

1

The Widening Police Family, Community Policing, and Police Culture

In order to understand the wider context into which Police Community Support Officers (PCSOs) were placed upon creation of the role in 2002, this chapter will explore three key themes in British policing and police research in the late twentieth and early twenty-first centuries: public sector pluralization, community policing, and the occupational culture in policing. These are the three elements of contemporary policing which have the most significant influence on the daily experiences of PCSOs, and they are the areas in which PCSOs themselves have been able to shape practice. The purpose of this book is thus to examine the effects of the pluralization of public policing within the context of community policing and the resultant shaping of the police occupational culture from these processes through the lived experiences of PCSOs. The pluralization of policing and, in particular, that of the public sector will be considered first.

Public Sector Pluralization

The pluralization of policing is a topic which has received a great deal of scholarly attention over many decades (see for example Shearing and Stenning 1983; Jones and Newburn 1998; Johnston and Shearing 2003; Crawford 2006; Wood and Shearing 2007; Zedner 2009). These discussions examine the growing role and influence of the private sector, as well as the diversification of the public sector, especially in the UK. The proliferation of actors, agencies, and the hybrid contractual arrangements which are increasingly commonplace in the policing and security fields have posed challenges for scholars in terms of how best to understand

Police Community Support Officers. First Edition. Megan O'Neill. © Megan O'Neill 2019. Published 2019 by Oxford University Press.

their relationships and their wider implications for the governance of security. In terms of relationships between the public and private sectors, debates have tended to oscillate around whether policing can be best understood in a 'nodal' framework (Johnston and Shearing 2003) or as 'anchored pluralism' (Loader and Walker 2006). The 'nodal' model describes policing as a network of policing and security actors and agencies which coalesce at key points, or 'nodes'. Not all nodes will have the same composition because they are structured by the particular security actors relevant to that area. Within this formulation, no one provider or sector is given prominence over another. This poses a challenge for the often-assumed pre-eminence of the state in matters of security in that all actors, the state included, operate in horizontal relationships with no one player having a larger role than any other. For the 'anchored pluralism' approach, the public police are seen as the most significant player in the plural policing field, as they hold the symbolic authority and command that actors in the private sector do not. For Loader and other colleagues, there is a clear normative message in their work, in that only the public police can truly protect and advance the public good and thus must serve as an 'anchor' for the others. The writers in the nodal field would argue that the public police are given undo prominence in these discussions, irrespective of who 'should' be doing policing in a democratic society (White 2012).

While these discourses have featured prominently in contemporary policing debates about plurality, there have been challenges to them. Scholars in countries out with the UK or the USA argue that the plurality of policing in other nations is not following the same path as the Anglo-American model, in that the private sector occupies a much smaller and far less significant position in policing arrangements. For example, Terpstra (2017) argues that in Austria, owing to its political history, deeply embedded fears remain of distributing policing authority across too wide a range of actors. The state is viewed as the only truly 'secure' source of policing authority and governance, which has meant that the private sector occupies a very small role in Austrian policing and security arrangements. Terpstra argues that this is far more than 'nostalgia', as Shearing and Wood (2003) might suggest. Likewise, Devroe (2017) describes how the multilayered policing arrangements in Belgium, while markedly different in this respect from Austria, also have positioned the state as the only secure source of policing and the guardians of social peace. This arrangement has developed from decades of political strife and historical corruption scandals, resulting in an uneasy compromise that cannot be trusted to any actor or agency out with the state. Devroe argues that the primary issue is not about the role of government (Loader and Walker) nor structures of governance (Johnston, Shearing, and Crawford), as the existing Anglo-American discourses position the debate. For Belgium, it is about the power relations inherent in the regulation of society and how best to maintain these in a complex political compromise.

Partnership working

While the role of the private sector is of course important to consider in discussions of the diversification of contemporary security and policing, the public sector itself has also experienced significant diversification in recent years. Analysis of the pluralization of the public sector in Britain, and mainly in England and Wales, often begins with the Crime and Disorder Act 1998 (CDA 1998) which introduced new mandates for collaborative working. While collaborative working had been taking place informally before the CDA 1998, this was the first time it had been mandated in legislation in England and Wales. The police were now obligated by law to work with other organizations, such as the health service, fire service, youth services, housing services, and educational services, to address issues of safety and security in local areas. These partnerships occur in a variety of formats: among the most significant (for the police at least) are Crime and Disorder Reduction Partnerships, also known as Community Safety Partnerships. Police work with partners largely in the context of community, or 'Neighbourhood', policing, but partners are also encountered in other arenas of police work (such as in traffic policing). There is a good deal of literature about the early years of these partnerships which documents many problems and obstacles to effective working (see for example Blagg et al 1988; Sampson et al 1988; Crawford 1997). One of the issues sighted most often is incompatible occupational cultures. The police were regarded as hijacking partnerships for their own ends (crime control rather than 'safety'), dominating meetings rather than being an equal partner, and losing patience with other organizations whose internal processes did not react to requests for assistance or shared resources as quickly as the police would have liked (Edwards 2002; Matthews et al 2007). The police were seen as struggling to work in the short-term with focused attention and in planning longer-term interventions (Pearson et al 1992). Since this time, however, collaborative working, or 'co-production', (Osborne and Strokosch 2013) has become commonplace within policing and the public sector more widely. Prior to the retraction of public sector funding brought in by the Coalition Government in 2010, there were signs that (in some jurisdictions at least) the police and their partners had overcome many of the early hurdles of partnership work and had found ways to utilize the strengths of each other's agencies (O'Neill and McCarthy 2014). This has included initiatives such as co-location, where representatives of all the relevant agencies will share office space in order to enhance communication and collaboration. However, since 2010, many areas of the public sector have been subject to a significant reduction in funding, and this has had an impact on the composition and reach of public sector partnerships, in that staff no longer have as much time or resources to offer these arrangements (O'Neill 2014a), despite collaboration being identified as a means to saving expenditure by Her Majesty's Inspectorate of Constabulary (2014).

Other policing actors

In addition to mandating greater collaboration between existing actors in the public sector through the CDA 1998, the New Labour government also developed new roles at the municipal level for policing and safety. A neighbourhood wardens scheme was proposed by the Social Exclusion Unit in 1998, and in May 2000, a Neighbourhood Wardens Unit was established in the Department of the Environment, Transport and the Regions, to take the project forward with government support and funding (Jacobsen and Saville 1999; Social Exclusion Unit 2001). The intention of the scheme was primarily to provide an authoritative presence in low-income areas to reduce crime and fear of crime. The remit of wardens broadened over time and, in some cases, beyond residential areas. In a review of the scheme, Jacobsen and Saville (1999) find that the three main areas of work for neighbourhood wardens were crime prevention, environmental improvements, and community development. In Crawford's (2006) analysis of wardens in

Leeds, he suggests that in areas with a history of distrust towards the police, wardens provided a more trustworthy connection to public services. At the time of his research,[1] there were about 250 schemes operating in the UK. Scotland introduced its community wardens scheme in 2004, after a review of a pilot scheme which operated between 2002 and 2003. Since that time, there have been over 500 community wardens positions filled in Scotland (Brown 2017).

Some community wardens, as well as other non-police security actors from both the public and the private sector, became registered as 'accredited officers'. This role was one of the elements of the Police Reform Act (2002), and it allows chief constables to establish local schemes that empower appropriate local agents to issue fixed penalty notices for disorder, as well as other low-level policing support functions. These individuals are meant to be suitability qualified and trained but will not be employees of the police (Crawford et al 2005). As such, the police are able to retain some degree of control over the work of individuals who do police-type work but are not themselves police officers (Crawford 2006). The last time a national audit was taken of the accreditation scheme, there were just over 2,200 people employed as accredited officers across England and Wales (Home Office 2011). The numbers in any one scheme range from 1 to 100. The Police Reform Act (2002) also introduced the role of 'designated officers', who are employed by police forces to do specialist tasks with relevant powers, such as Investigation Officers, Detention Officers, or Escort Officers (Mawby and Wright 2008). As of September 2015, there are just over 4,200 designated officers in the police forces of England and Wales (Hargreaves 2016).[2]

Police Community Support Officers

The discussion above has shown that the range of actors involved in policing in the public sector is wide. However, one key group

[1] There is not a great deal of research on community wardens in England and Wales. As they are employed by local authorities, calculating their total number is difficult.

[2] This situation began changing with the introduction of the Policing and Crime Act (2017). This will be explored further in Chapter 7.

has yet to be discussed, and this group was introduced in the Police Reform Act (2002): PCSOs. PCSOs are a type of policing auxiliary: salaried members of support staff without the warranted power of arrest,[3] but who provide a visible patrol presence as part of Neighbourhood Policing Teams (NPTs) (Home Office 2001; ACPO 2007). They are loosely based on the 'police patroller' model of the Netherlands, which is part of the formal police rank structure in a tier below that of a full constable.[4] While police patrollers do have the warranted power of arrest and carry handcuffs and a baton, their main tasks are to patrol neighbourhoods on foot, to respond to questions from the public, and to maintain order (Hofstra and Shapland 1997; Hauber et al 1996). PCSOs in England and Wales are intended to focus on community engagement and reassurance, with limited powers to enable them to address anti-social behaviour and low-level crime. The Police Reform Act (2002) conferred a range of powers to all PCSOs but also included specific additional powers that were at the discretion of the local Chief Constable to grant to his or her staff, should local need require them.[5] In several police forces, PCSOs were granted the ability to detain a person for up to half an hour while awaiting the arrival of a police officer. In the main, however, the role of a PCSO is focused on visible foot patrol, community engagement, and attending to nuisance issues (Cooper et al 2006; ACPO 2007). While, initially, their numbers rose steadily after their implementation, PCSOs have been targeted for efficiency savings by many police forces after the 20% reduction in funding to policing following the arrival of the Coalition Government in 2010 (Millie 2013). PCSOs, as members of police staff, can be made redundant and are thus particularly vulnerable during periods of austerity. At their height in 2010, they numbered approximately 16,900 (Greig-Midlane 2014). By September 2017,

[3] As with any member of the public, PCSOs have both the citizen's power of arrest and the use of reasonable force as stipulated by sections 2 and 3 of the Criminal Law Act 1967. However, in the course of the research to be discussed here, it was found that supervisors discouraged PCSOs from using these powers, as it would unduly confuse the boundaries between them and police constables, both for themselves and for members of the public.

[4] The 'police patroller' role in the Netherlands has now largely disappeared, owing to their marginal position within the police (van Steden 2017).

[5] This is another situation which has changed in light of the Policing and Crime Act (2017), and it will be discussed further in Chapter 7.

there were 10,200 PCSOs in England and Wales (Home Office 2017), a drop of 40%. Greig-Midlane (2014) argues that this has resulted in a significant reduction in neighbourhood policing capacity for most police forces. This issue will be explored in more detail later in the book.

When PCSOs were first introduced in 2002 (before the introduction of neighbourhood policing), there was a great deal of confusion over what they were meant to do, both externally among the public and internally within police forces, as well as how they would fit into the police service, both practically and culturally. While their uniforms are deliberately similar to their police officer counterparts to enhance their legitimacy in the minds of the public (Cooke 2005), this can also cause confusion as to their purpose and level of authority. Johnston (2005, 2006, and 2007) explores the experiences of PCSOs in London in the early days of their implementation. He finds that training for PCSOs was insufficient in preparing them for the role, and their supervision arrangements were unclear. Sergeants and inspectors had little guidance on assimilating PCSOs into existing operational and managerial structures. It is unsurprising that PCSOs in Johnston's research did not feel they were part of the police 'family' and that many were on disciplinary charges because of lack of guidance and support as to what was expected of them as employees. PCSOs, however, do tend to be a more diverse group than their police officer counterparts in terms of ethnicity and gender, as Johnston (2005) also notes.

Other than Johnston's early research, most studies of PCSOs have tended to focus on their work and relationships in the wider community. For example, Merritt (2009, 2010) examines the outward-facing role of PCSOs, and whether they are adopting a community engagement–style approach (what he calls 'bridge builders'), or tend more towards an enforcement-focused 'junior' police officer role. He finds that PCSOs fall somewhere on a continuum between the two, but are tending more towards the 'junior enforcer' side. There are differing opinions within the police as to how confrontational and enforcement oriented PCSOs should be. Some feel this would hinder their ability to be links with the community (Paskell 2007), whereas others, including some PCSOs, feel that a degree of enforcement power is important in the community so that they can effectively address low-level disorder (Merritt 2010). Cosgrove and Ramshaw (2013) find that although

PCSOs have great potential to improve police relationships with the community, they tend to be used in (and are encouraged to adopt) a crime-control capacity, in contrast to the general community engagement intention behind their role. Using a survey of shopping centre customers, Rowland and Coupe (2014) find that while PCSOs engender more feelings of safety in the public than do security guards, they do not score as highly in this regard as police officers do.

With some exceptions (see for example Rogers 2017), discussions of 'plural policing' tend to frame the debate as concerning, on the one hand, fully paid, full-time uniformed police officers (of various ranks), and on the other, the multiple manifestations of the private or semiprivate sector. Crawford (2006) touches to an extent on the diversity within the public police when he discusses the *monopolistic* model of policing (as one of five co-existing models in the UK, with the others being *steering, networked, market*, and *private government*) in which the public police try to retain control of their remit through such things as the introduction of PCSOs. In this conception, the diversification of the public police provision is itself just one element of the larger and varied pluralization process. In a related discussion, Johnston (2005, 2007) addresses the concept of the 'police extended family', which tends to include hybrid models such as private sector agencies given accreditation by the public police. One of the few examples of research which explores the internal relationships in public policing since the arrival of PCSOs is that of Cosgrove (2015). She argues that, as police officers have been in the past (Reiner 2010), PCSOs can be understood through a system of typologies which reflect their levels of dedication, focus, and acceptance of their limited power. For Cosgrove, these are 'Frustrated', 'Disillusioned', and 'Professional' PCSOs. In general, however, when discussions touch on the nature of relationships within policing, this tends to be in relation to how the public police have reacted to a more developed and complex policing role played by the private sector in democratic countries and the degree to which the private sector is accepted as a legitimate partner in policing. What is often overlooked is a detailed study of the pluralization of the public police itself, as well as how that is experienced by the actors within it. This book will address that gap, within the specific context of community policing.

Community and Neighbourhood Policing

PCSOs represent the most recent effort in England and Wales to meet the public's insatiable demand for 'more Bobbies on the beat' (Hanson 2010; Utley 2010; Barrett 2013). As Loader and Mulcahy (2003) discover in their research, not only is the mythical local Bobby held as the epitome of policing *par excellence* worldwide, it has even come to represent for many an 'exemplar of English nationhood' itself (2003: 83), such is the prominence of the figure as an embodiment of security, morality, and community. The perceived loss of the Bobby signifies for many not only a loss of what was 'good' and 'right' about policing generally, but also the loss of an important feature of local community cohesion (Loader and Mulcahy 2003). Visible patrolling—exemplified by the Bobby (in the past) and PCSOs (more recently)—is often seen as the principle component of community policing (Wakefield 2006), which will be discussed next.

The development of community policing

Community policing as an explicit policing method was initially attempted in England and Wales in the 1980s and 1990s. This was to compensate for a transition in operational policing which occurred in the 1960s when police officers reduced foot patrols in favour of mobilized patrols in cars in order to respond to events more quickly and over a larger area. Despite the intention to improve community relations through this method, the opposite happened in that local officers became detached from their beat areas and its residents (O'Neill 2010). These early forays back into 'community policing' twenty years later are now regarded largely as failures. The effort was both piecemeal and not supported across the organization in any systematic way (Fielding 1995; Myhill and Quinton 2010). The main emphasis in policing, especially in the 1990s, was on efficiency and performance management structures. The police were to focus on a narrow set of tasks as being their core remit (mainly volume crime), and to demonstrate their effectiveness in these on a regular basis through targets (Home Office 1995; Innes et al 2004; Myhill and Quinton 2010). Both this type of work and performance measures do not allow for the more nebulous activity associated with community policing, which is not easily captured by quantitative instruments and targets. It was the New Labour government at the turn of the century who brought in another change of policing focus to answer concerns that it was too top-down in its approach to crime and community safety. The 'reassurance gap' had also been identified at this time, in that while overall crime rates were falling, general public concern about crime and about 'quality-of-life' issues were rising (Herrington and Millie 2006; Lowe and Innes 2012; Pratchett 2004; Bullock and Sindall 2014). The National Reassurance Policing Programme (NRPP) was piloted to assess whether strategies such as visible foot patrol and consultations with communities could not only address issues of crime and disorder but also start to reassure the public that they are safe (Fielding and Innes 2006; Barker 2014). This was eventually developed into neighbourhood policing[6] (in 2005), and it rolled out nationally in 2008. Each local area in England and Wales then had its own identifiable NPT comprised of community police officers, PCSOs, and Special Constables (Mason 2009).

Although community policing and neighbourhood policing can be difficult to define (Tilley 2008; O'Neill 2010), common elements include police focusing their operations at local levels, addressing issues unique to particular communities, community consensus guiding the police, policing being locally accountable, and police using their discretion to improve public confidence (Brogden and Nijhar 2005). It is in this type of policing method that PCSOs found their niche as the modern-day 'Bobby on the beat' (Caless 2007; Greig-Midlane 2014). A crucial component of neighbourhood policing in England and Wales, and of the theory on which the NRPP was based, 'signal crimes', is that members of local communities must be consulted about what issues matter to them most (Foster and Jones 2010; Barker 2014). The police are then to find ways to attend to these issues, and not just to the volume crimes, which had been the case previously. There is

[6] The use of the term *neighbourhood policing* instead of *community policing* in England and Wales was in part a political choice to encourage a geospatial identification with this type of policing. It was felt this would encourage a greater sense of ownership of the process in local residents who, while they may belong to a number of communities of interest, would only have one 'neighbourhood'. The idea was also to reflect a growing political focus on 'localism' through the enhanced role for residents in guiding the policing of their area (Innes 2005).

some evidence to suggest that neighbourhood policing is correlated with an increase in public confidence in the police, as well as with a reduction in the public's assessment of local crime levels (Myhill and Quinton 2010; Wood et al 2014), which suggests that attending to the low-level issues which matter in the day-to-day experiences of community members can have an impact on their views of both the police and their own safety. However, while the literature on neighbourhood policing is largely favourable, it does mention that the method can be difficult to get right (Foster and Jones 2010; Lowe and Innes 2012). For example, Foster and Jones (2010) find that many officers and staff in the area they studied had underestimated the importance of consulting with community members and groups. These officers did not have a good understanding of the composition of their communities, what the concerns of their community were, or how best to communicate with and report on police actions in the area. This undermined the purpose of the community policing approach there. Wood et al (2014), in their study of directed foot patrols in crime 'hot spot' areas, report that while officers did indeed gain a much deeper understanding of the local residents, their internal relationships (e.g. that not everyone was 'up to' something), and the social problems for that area, the officers also became frustrated with both their inability to change these conditions and the boredom they experienced with their limited beat range. However, the authors did concede that this might have been due to the patrols being conducted by new recruits to the police who had not yet experienced the more action-oriented aspects of the role, which they were keen to do.

Community policing and fiscal restraint

Despite limitations within community policing, it is still regarded as a core component of contemporary police work. In England and Wales, it has been argued to be not only an important policing method but an entire policing philosophy which has revolutionized the public police service (Home Office 2004; Home Office 2005; Foster and Jones 2010). However, neighbourhood policing developed in England and Wales at a time when police forces were experiencing year-on-year increases in their officer and staff numbers. Neighbourhood policing is a resource-intensive activity, but it was manageable within these growing numbers. What has transpired since the change of government in 2010, and the imposition of a 20% reduction in funding for policing, is an overall retraction in the numbers of police officers and staff in most police forces. This has required senior staff to reconsider the deployment of their shrinking resources. In the main, the percentage of the police workforce occupied by PCSOs has remained largely constant. However, with fewer of them and of their police officer counterparts, there is less time available for the types of community police work which were the norm under the New Labour government, such as visible patrols and community engagement activities (Greig-Midlane 2014; Longstaff et al 2015; Higgins 2018). A review of police effectiveness by Her Majesty's Inspectorate of Constabulary (HMIC) in 2015 finds that many police forces were abstracting their neighbourhood police officers into other tasks such as response or crime investigation, which meant that the preventative work often associated with neighbourhood policing was reducing (HMIC 2016). Millie (2013) argues that it is perhaps time to reconsider the range of tasks and roles in which the police are involved, and try to reallocate these to other agencies and actors, such as leading disaster management or stewarding large events. However, while it is not always directly related to 'cutting crime' (May 2011), neighbourhood policing is a method by which the police fulfil their remit to maintain order, and thus it has its place in the current police mandate (Banton 1964; Ericson 1982; Millie 2013). The Police Foundation (Longstaff et al 2015) has warned against using economics to determine the mandate for policing, which they argue should instead be based on a clear strategy, including long-term policing goals such as those exemplified in neighbourhood policing. This can include trust building in communities, as well as identifying early signs of risk in certain groups (such as poor parenting or mental ill health). To focus too narrowly on the 'crime-cutting' side of the police role, it is argued, is short-sighted and ultimately self-defeating in terms of building opportunities for crime prevention (Longstaff et al 2015).[7] A fuller

[7] The College of Policing (2018) has developed Neighbourhood Policing Guidelines based on an assessment of existing research and practice, which support these and other arguments about what neighbourhood policing 'should' be. These can be accessed here: http://www.college.police.uk/What-we-do/Support/Guidelines/Neighbourhood-Policing/Pages/default.aspx.

discussion of the current state and future of community policing will be taken up in the book's conclusion.

Doing neighbourhood policing

When neighbourhood policing was fully rolled out across England and Wales in 2008, NPTs (or other similar titles, such as 'Safer Neighbourhood Teams') were the primary unit through which this type of policing was carried out. They were comprised of several types of policing actors, the primary ones being community police officers and their supervisors (sergeants and inspectors). These officers were intended to be restricted to community policing only and not to be abstracted into other areas of police work, such as response policing. PCSOs were also key components of NPTs, whose role it was (and still is) to support the work of the community police officers by undertaking tasks that do not require a warranted police officer. These are activities such as giving out crime prevention advice, going door to door to warn of a risk of burglary to the area, attending community events, and so on. Special Constables are also involved in community policing to a degree (see Bullock and Leeney 2014), as and when the need arises. These volunteer officers also support the work of the regular community officers, such as in special operations, to address a particular crime problem. NPTs in some areas benefitted from dedicated support staff who would address the 'back office' organizational tasks, such as organizing team briefings and preparing community newsletters. Finally, NPTs work on a regular basis with other members of the public and, to some extent, private sectors to develop coordinated approaches to community problems.

Each NPT had its own 'neighbourhood' area for which it was responsible. The size of the neighbourhoods, or beat units, varied from one police force to another and within police forces, depending on the population and the geography of the area. Within these areas, the NPTs were to focus on engagement with communities, problem-solving approaches, and high visibility activities (such as foot patrol). The aims were to build public confidence in the police, reassure the public that they were safe, and reduce crime (Longstaff et al 2015). Working in partnership with other public (and private sector) agencies was an important part of this work, as was building mechanisms by which to keep local communities informed of police activities and to seek their guidance and feedback. Sir Ronnie Flanagan conducted a review of neighbourhood policing in 2007 and found that while demonstrable progress had been made, areas in need of significant development remained. In particular, he singled out the need for the police to work fully in partnership with other agencies in order to have coordinated service delivery and to best achieve problem-solving (Flanagan 2008). He called for a 'Neighbourhood Management' approach, which would involve the creation of multiagency teams, preferably co-located and led by a neighbourhood manager. This would include joint performance measurements and a pooling of resources and budgets. Flanagan (2008) acknowledged that this approach would present a challenge to traditional police methods of working and other 'cultural hurdles' in terms of the degree of openness required to enable this type of collaboration. While some police areas were able to implement neighbourhood management to a degree, before the change in government in 2010, Flanagan's acknowledgement of the cultural challenge this presented was accurate. It is to a more detailed look at research on the police occupational culture, especially in relation to community policing and partnership working, that we now turn.

Police Culture Research

Research into the occupational culture of the police has a long history in social science, especially in the USA and the UK. Early work in the 1950s and 1960s tended to discuss issues related to police discretion (see for example Westley 1970; Bittner 1967; Banton 1964) because of the contentious role of the police in the civil rights movement of the time. Research on the police then moved from a civil libertarian investigation of police powers to a social interactionist analysis of policing as performance (see especially Manning 1977; Van Maanen 1975, 1978). Policing was no longer regarded as an objective task to be achieved, but as an ongoing, interactive process which is refined, tested, and rehearsed continuously (McCarthy 2014). Analyses at that time identified common elements of a police occupational culture such as insularity, suspicion, solidarity, and an action-focused work ethic (Reiner 2010). Later work in this field examines how it might be more appropriate to look at police *cultures*, as a variety of manifestations have been documented (Paoline 2003; Cockcroft 2013). For example, Reuss-Ianni (1983) looks at differences between the ranks; Muir (1977) and Reiner (1978) explore various police officer typologies; and Cain (1971) examines differences between urban and rural officers. Other research discusses the complexity of the occupational culture in policing, such as Chan's (1996) examination of the interplay between wider social and political forces and police culture. Sklansky (2007) argues that while some elements of the police experience remain constant over time, and in different places, a police 'subculture' is an unhelpful and outdated idea, so much so that it is hindering attempts at reform of the police in the USA. Waddington (1999) argues that researchers have overplayed the significance of police officer 'banter' for decades, as well as its role in determining police practice. However, work by Loftus (2009) points to the difficulty of changing informal police practice, and argues that despite the many reforms brought about by the Lawrence Report (Macpherson 1999), the 'classic' elements of police culture as described in the 1950s and 1960s remains in evidence.

For the purposes of this text, the discussion to follow will focus on elements of police culture, identified through research, which have particular relevance for an examination of the pluralization of public sector policing. This will include bonding and alienation, storytelling, 'soft' or 'social work' policing, action orientation, and issues to do with gender and ethnicity. The full police culture 'cannon' has been examined in more detail elsewhere (such as Cockcroft 2013; Loftus 2009; Paoline 2003; Chan 1997), and these texts provide a more comprehensive discussion of the topic and related literature.

Bonding and alienation

While police officers may come to the role from a variety of backgrounds, political orientations, and demographics, the policing task itself tends to present common experiences and stresses, such as working unsociable hours, being exposed to human suffering and violence, and a constant wariness of the unseen threat (Skolnick 1994; Paoline 2003; Reiner 2010). One of the methods of coping with these challenges which researchers have regularly identified is a tendency for police officers to bond together through a strong sense of group loyalty, while also isolating themselves from 'outsiders'. This stems from a need to rely on each other in difficult situations but can also involve protecting fellow officers from scrutiny and investigation (Westley 1970; Skolnick and Fyfe 1993). Those on the outside of the police group can range from the public to others in the public services to senior police officers. Typologies have been identified that some police groups use to categorize those on the outside, which emphasize their position as 'them' compared to the police 'us' (Loftus 2009). For example, 'police property' (Reiner 2010) is used for the lowest in society with whom no one else wants to engage, such as drug addicts, vagrants, or alcoholics. Holdaway (1983) notes the categories of 'challengers', 'disarmers', and 'do-gooders'. Challengers can penetrate the barriers of the police organization and reveal its secrets (such as doctors, lawyers, social workers, or researchers). Disarmers are the socially vulnerable who tend to illicit public sympathy, such as children or the elderly. Do-gooders tend to be political activists, often anti-police, who make the policing job more difficult. Differences in occupational orientation have been noted between the ranks (most notably by Reuss-Ianni 1983), which can mean that the lower ranks do not trust the higher ranks to protect them and regard them in effect as outsiders.

Consideration has also been given to relationships between the public police and those of the private sector (Stenning 1989; Wakefield 2003), and research has found a variety of police perspectives towards this group (Gill 2015). This has ranged from outright hostility to grudging acceptance and even to effective collaboration. Police forces themselves can, in the right circumstances, 'sell' their services for a fee (such as when policing inside football grounds; see O'Neill 2005) or outsource their roles (such as for guarding duties; see White 2015 for an analysis), demonstrating the complexity of the public–private divide (White 2012). As the section above on partnership working demonstrated, over time, the police have demonstrated a greater willingness to collaborate with the 'outsider' organizations, those which just a few years ago would have been regarded as a threat (Holdaway's 'challengers'; see also Flanagan 2008). Police forces in the early years of the twenty-first century were not only mandated by law to collaborate with other organizations, but would actively seek out and build relationships with public sector workers (O'Neill and McCarthy 2014). There were varieties of reasons for this, some more self-serving than others (such as a desire to shift problematic cases to other agencies). The fact remains, however, that by the time of the public sector fiscal restraint in 2010, partnership work in policing was a commonplace activity, which, in many areas, was openly welcomed and encouraged (McCarthy and O'Neill 2014).

The wide variation which has been noted over time in the relationships between the police, the public sector agencies, and other security actors, as well as the historical tendency on the part of the police to turn inwards when under threat, will be important for latter discussions of how rank-and-file police officers in England and Wales adjusted to the arrival of PCSOs in the early 2000s. While private security and other public sector agents will always be on the 'outside' of the public police circle, the picture is less clear for PCSOs. They are employed by police forces and they work directly with police officers in community policing, but, as members of support staff, they are not always regarded by police officers as part of 'us'. Adaptations to this new occupational arrangement will be explored later in this book.

Storytelling

Research into police culture, informal practice, and in-group bonding has also noted the importance of storytelling in policing. Discussion here has tended to oscillate between two different perspectives, which present varying degrees of emphasis on the extent to which stories and storytelling influence the work of police officers in practice. Ethnographers such as Van Maanen (1973), Manning (1977), Punch (1979), and van Hulst (2013) write in detail about the stories they encountered in their research and the role these played in subsequent police practice. Shearing and Ericson (1991) argue that policing discourse is constitutive of police work, and for them this is not in a direct, linear sense in terms of 'how to handle this situation', but rather on a cognitive level, to reveal how the world works. They identified different types of stories which are told in different types of contexts, but each serves a purpose in passing on the general knowledge of policing. The value of police stories is not in their 'truth' (which is often questionable) but in their role in developing the craft of policing.

For other scholars, notably Fielding (1994) and Waddington (1999), police storytelling has been overemphasized in policing research. Waddington sees the role of storytelling as no more than a mechanism to release tension, to rebuild images of policing as an exciting occupation, and to perform in front of colleagues. He sees no connection between what the police say and what the police do, and warns other scholars against assuming a link connecting these. For Waddington (1999) stories that the police tell in their backstage areas (Goffman 1959) do not match the reality of policing. Smith and Grey (1985) also find similar patterns in their study of racist language in the Metropolitan Police. While they overheard multiple racist epithets used during the course of their observations when police officers were away from the public, they did not detect any noticeable difference in the way that these officers interacted with ethnic minorities in the course of their duties.

van Hulst (2013), in a study of storytelling in police backstage spaces, argues for a middle ground between these theoretical positions. Following the argument of Shearing and Ericson (1991), van Hulst postulates that context is important when studying the role of stories and storytelling in policing. The space in which the story is told, the type of story, its length, and the relationship between the listeners: all of these variables are significant in determining the purpose of the story. Different types of stories do different work, and not all of them are dramatic 'war' stories of action or bravery for the purposes of performance (although some are). For van Hulst (2013) there does have to be a value to the story, a 'tellability', in order for it to be recounted, but this is not solely determined by its dramatic merits. Some stories are indeed told only to be the 'repair shop' (Waddington 1999) of policing, but others will have a more cognitive discourse in order to pass on the lessons of experiential learning in policing. van Hulst (2013) argues that police storytelling is more social practice than political, and is a crucial part of police work. It is through stories, some dramatic, some mundane, some factual, that the experience of policing practice is shared and developed (see also van Hulst 2017). As emerged from the study of PCSOs in England, storytelling is indeed an important element of their working lives, as well as that of their police officer colleagues. So much so that Chapter 6 of this book will argue that storytelling is a crucial component in the process of police occupational culture development for both PCSOs and police officers.

'Soft' policing

As PCSOs are intended to be community facing and to avoid confrontation whenever possible, their role speaks to another aspect of the police culture literature, that of the extent to which policing is a 'soft' activity—rather than a 'hard' crime-fighting one—and it questions which activity is the more valued. Innes (2005) defines *soft policing* as 'the non-coercive aspects of police-led social control encompassing the provision of a visible presence of authority, persuasion, negotiation and community interaction' (2005: 157). Recent discussions around 'soft' policing in England and Wales are often linked to the development of neighbourhood policing in the early 2000s. McCarthy (2014) has a slightly different viewpoint from Innes on the exact nature of soft policing and argues that while there is a degree of overlap between soft policing styles and neighbourhood policing, they are not the same thing. Neighbourhood policing is primarily concerned with building relationships and trust between the police and citizens, which is not a focus for soft policing. The latter policing method is focused more upon identifying those 'at risk' of offending, or who are vulnerable in some way, and putting in place interventions to reduce their risk of harm (either to themselves or to others). This often entails multiagency work between the police and other groups in the public sector, and here is where overlap with neighbourhood policing can be found (McCarthy 2014). While soft policing and neighbourhood policing both have preventative and multiagency methodologies, their orientations are slightly different in that one is far wider than the other is.

Historically, 'soft' styles of policing have been identified as important complementary elements within police practice, to counteract the influence of the more reactive policing styles. Fielding (1995) points out that softer methods are useful in drawing out community intelligence which can assist in the 'hard' crime-control activities. Muir (1977) argues using only force and not using negotiation and persuasion in policing to achieve desired ends was a policing failure. Under New Labour in the 2000s, soft policing was formally identified as a key element of police reform and, ultimately, as a style of policing that the public valued highly (Innes 2005; McCarthy 2014). Decades of police culture research, however, describes how difficult it is to convince police officers of the merits of soft policing, as officers tend to value work which is more reactive and oriented around 'action', such as pursuing offenders. The next section will develop this in more detail.

Action orientation

Despite research and official policy which emphasizes the importance of a blend of policing styles, much of the 'classic' police culture research finds that it was in the moments of 'action' and 'crime fighting' that the police felt most fulfilled in their practice. Prior to the introduction of neighbourhood policing in England and Wales in the early 2000s, community policing was often regarded (internally) as the lowest form of police work. This was the job to which police officers were sent as a punishment or when on the eve of retirement, as it is perceived to lack the potential for action, danger, and excitement more prevalent in response policing, which police officers tend to value (Reiner 1978; Van Maanen 1978; Holdaway 1983; Smith and Gray 1985; Marks 2005; Loftus 2009). Cultural orientations around community policing began to change in the early years of the twenty-first century (O'Neill 2014a). Even so, the draw of 'blue lights' calls was difficult to resist for community officers, including PCSOs, during the course of the research project to be explored in this book. Scholars from the social interactionist period of police research attribute this love of action and 'crime fighting' to a strong sense of mission often detected among police officers (Reiner 2010). Manning (1997: 261) explores this through the 'threat-danger-hero' mythology of policing, whereby the potential for danger and uncertainty in the role is elevated to a core element of its ideology. According to Manning, these elements which provide the most satisfaction for police officers—and keep them dedicated to an occupation that otherwise is largely uneventful and even monotonous at times—comprise less than 10% of police patrols. The heroic 'crime-fighter' imagery is sold to the public as one of the main purposes of policing, and this is reinforced internally through its centrality to police promotions and awards processes, as well as to praise from colleagues.

The symbolic, if not entirely realistic, importance of danger and uncertainty in policing is reflected in Skolnick's concept of the 'symbolic assailant' (1994: 44). Police officers are instructed from the start of their training (both formal and informal) to constantly be watchful and observant in order to detect as early as possible potentially dangerous or threatening individuals. Over time, through their own experiential learning and from collecting the stories of others, police officers develop a shorthand for detecting threats. This could be the way a person walks, his or her appearance, the way he or she speaks, and the wider context in which the person is encountered. These signs coalesce as the 'symbolic assailant' and provide the police with a mechanism for detecting danger (Crank 2004). As the policing profession has developed as one based on an ideology of danger, uncertainty, and the need for heroic action, in its understandable that this has also lead to a degree of suspicion of the wider public, any one of whom could embody one or more the symbolic assailant's characteristics (Cockcroft 2013). The problem is that the mundane reality of policing eventually infringes on the action-oriented mythology, which can leave some police officers to be dispirited and cynical (Manning 1997). Thus while the relatively few action-oriented and 'crime-fighting' elements of policing have attracted many to the role and work, to retain those who are there, it has contributed to a situation where the 'softer' and more negotiation-based aspects of policing have traditionally been played down or even rejected, despite their centrality to police work. As PCSOs were created primarily to attend to this aspect of policing in a community context, it is not surprising that they have experienced ongoing challenges to be taken seriously as legitimate members of public policing teams in England and Wales. This daily struggle for PCSOs to gain legitimacy internally will be developed later in the book.

Gender and ethnicity

Closely linked to the value placed on danger and excitement in police work is the cultural emphasis on the masculine nature of policing, also documented in many studies (Martin 1980; Smith and Gray 1985; Hunt 1990; Fielding 1994; Martin 1996; Brown and Heidensohn 2000; Silvestri 2003; Westmarland 2001). In these conceptualizations, women police officers are ill-equipped to handle 'real' policing and will often find themselves in 'softer' roles, such as family-liaison work or domestic violence cases, and experience difficulty in gaining entry to specialisms such as firearms, detective work, or public order units (Bryant et al 1985; Fielding and Fielding 1992; Brown et al 1993). Research that is more recent suggests that this may be changing to a degree (Westmarland 2001). There are now more women in policing and in senior roles. However, Silvestri (2003) argues that this has not resulted in a clear change in the occupational culture, as hard work is still valued as the main route to success, placing women at a disadvantage, as they are more likely to have had periods away from work or difficulty in accessing the range of policing experiences open to men.

Minority ethnic members of the police service have also experienced difficulties in gaining full acceptance by their police officer colleagues. Research (such as that of Holdaway and Barron 1997; Martin 1994; Holdaway and O'Neill 2004) describes how black and other minority ethnic police officers have been subject to overt or covert discrimination, isolation, and bullying within their police organizations. This has been the case in both the UK and the USA (Skolnick 1994; Rowe 2004). Black and minority ethnic officers report finding it more difficult to be promoted or to join specialisms, to have claims of discrimination taken seriously, and to fit into police social circles (Holdaway and O'Neill 2004; Holdaway and O'Neill 2006; Rowe 2004). This has led some officers in the UK to form staff support organizations, such as Black Police Associations (BPAs). While BPAs are not unions and thus not legally representative of staff views, they have been included in some senior management committees in police forces, and, until the funding cuts of 2010, they had their own budgets and dedicated resources. They are often consulted by senior managers on issues of ethnicity in policing and will support their members in claims of employment discrimination (Holdaway and O'Neill 2004; Holdaway and O'Neill 2006). BPAs were not initially welcomed by senior management, and they reported years of struggle to gain acceptance. The publication of the Stephen Lawrence Report in 1999 (Macpherson 1999) changed this landscape completely. In the Lawrence Report, Sir William Macpherson accuses policing organizations in England and Wales of institutional racism, which was displayed in the lack of care and due process shown by the Metropolitan Police in the murder investigation of black teenager, Stephen Lawrence, in 1993. This report represents a step change in approaches to racism in police practice, which, up until this point, was usually attributed to failures of individuals (Scarman 1982; Holdaway and O'Neill 2004; Rowe 2004). Now the entire policing organization would be held to account for both its formal policies and practices and the net outcome of informal cultural practices in the treatment of minority ethnic groups both within and outside the police (for a critique see Souhami 2014).

In the years since the Lawrence Report was published, significant changes can be noted in policies and practices (at the very least in the formal sense) related to the policing of diverse communities and the experiences of black and minority ethnic police officers (Loftus 2009). Police forces are under intense political and media scrutiny in this regard, such that now, the rate at which police employ individuals from minority backgrounds is closely monitored, as is the ethnicity of people with whom the police interact in official capacities (such as stop and search and arrests). Black and minority ethnic officers, staff, and members of the public are more acutely aware than ever of their rights to equal treatment, which is in keeping with a broader shift in contemporary society towards an era of identity politics (Reiner 2010; Loftus 2009). As noted above, similar shifts in the experiences of women in policing have also been noted, and the needs of women as victims of crime (such as in cases of domestic violence) are taken more seriously (Heidensohn 2008). As the demographics of PCSOs might suggest, however, barriers remain in terms of these groups fully accessing employment as police officers or considering work as a police officer as appealing. Johnston (2005, 2006) notes that PCSOs have a greater representation of women and members of black and minority ethnic groups than do police constables and the other police ranks. While not all PCSOs wish to become regular police officers (as will be discussed later), this does suggest that the PCSO role is more welcoming for those usually excluded from the police ranks, and it speaks to the cultural representation of PCSO work not being 'real' policing.

Conclusion

Pluralization in policing, community policing, and manifestations of police culture are core aspects of the wider policing context into which PCSOs arrived in 2002. While police officers in many of the earlier studies of occupational culture were not found to value community policing and other types of soft policing methods often assigned to female officers (e.g. partnership work; see McCarthy 2014), this method was to revolutionize policing in England and Wales in the twenty-first century (Home Office 2004;

Home Office 2005; Foster and Jones 2010). As community policing developed and was embedded in police strategy and management, ever more aspects of 'police' work were undertaken by other actors in both the public and private sectors. These movements have seen what was once an insular and guarded organization develop into one which, in many ways (although not all), is more open to collaboration with outsiders and seems to better appreciate the 'social work' side of the policing task than was the case even twenty years ago. However, it could be argued that collaborating with those who are clearly outside of the police 'family' is less threatening than it is to embrace those now within it, such as PCSOs. As employees of police forces with a police-like mandate, these staff could be seen to present a greater danger to job security and the 'purity' of the police officer's role than would youth workers or CCTV operators. The next chapter of this book will describe the research project on which this text is based, a long-term observational study of PCSOs in community policing. The findings from this work then will be discussed in Section 2, which will consider how police officers and staff in six NPTs adapted to the challenges of working in a pluralized public policing environment, in terms of both their formal practice and their informal cultural orientations.

2

Researching Police Community Support Officers in England and Wales

This chapter will examine the research project on which this book is based and the theoretical framework used in the analysis. As this was an observational study of Police Community Support Officers (PCSOs), it is important to have a detailed understanding of the immediate context in which the work was conducted. Differences in the composition of the neighbourhood teams, the interior spaces within which PCSOs worked, the areas they patrolled, and the overall rhythm of their day will all have a bearing on the relationships which developed between PCSOs, their police officer colleagues, and members of the public (to be discussed in Part II of the book). Observational studies of the police are not new, with some of the most influential policing research to date coming from ethnographies (Banton 1964; Westley 1970; Cain 1973; Van Maanen 1973; Manning 1977; Marks 2004; Loftus 2009). The chapter begins with an overview of the methods which were employed in the study. Next, the six neighbourhood policing teams (NPTs) which were observed are described in detail to provide the context to the research. The chapter concludes with a discussion of Erving Goffman's 'dramaturgy', which provided a key theoretical framework for this analysis.

Methods Used in the Research

The methods used in this study of PCSOs follow those of earlier researchers of policing. Dating back to at least the 1950s with Westley's (1970) research, direct observation of the police has been regarded as an important way to understand not only what the police do, but how they do it and why. When a focus on symbolic interactionism developed in the 1970s, writers such as Manning (1977) and Van Maanen (1975, 1978) demonstrated that through in-depth observations of the police the symbolic significance of the social world of policing was revealed. This was only achieved through extended periods in the field so that rapport could be developed with police officers. Policing presents a usually impenetrable exterior to the outside world, and only once trust has been established with an 'outsider' are the informal and symbolic layers revealed (Reiner 2000). Many significant observational studies of policing have followed, such as Holdaway (1983), Fielding (1988), Marks (2005), and Loftus (2009). These studies are ethnographies, in that they present not only in-depth observations of a group over time, but also other related and simultaneous methods such as interviewing, note taking, collecting documents, and audio or visual recordings (Falzon 2009). The project discussed in this book, while drawing on this rich ethnographic research tradition, presents two departures from the existing police ethnography cannon. First of all, the participants in this research were not police officers, but police *staff*. As PCSOs do not hold the office of constable, they do not have the power of arrest or a legitimate use of force. However, as they present a public sector policing presence in local communities, wear a uniform, and undertake long periods of foot patrol, in addition to being members of the local NPT, it is justifiable to draw on ethnographic studies of warranted police officers as the wider context for this research.

The second departure which this project presents from existing police ethnographies is that it was conducted over multiple sites. Ethnographies in the traditional sense are usually in-depth studies of a group or social phenomenon over an extended period and within a specific (often clearly bounded) space (Bryman 2001; Falzon 2009). In the case of police ethnographies, this has meant that researchers restrict themselves to one police force and often to one team or area unit within that force (see e.g. Young 1991; Fielding 1993; Loftus 2009; and for an example of PCSOs, Cosgrove 2011 and 2015). This choice of a single site may not always be a deliberate one as access to the police for research purposes is notoriously difficult. In addition, observations of one site or social group does allow for a detailed understanding of social relations within it and the symbolic meanings attached to daily life which may not be apparent from brief field visits or interviews alone. However, policing is a social process that is significantly context dependent (Cain 1973; Herbert 1997; Fyfe 1991). Therefore, a methodological decision needed to be made between developing a detailed understanding of one group of PCSOs or sacrificing a degree of depth with one group to gather a more general understanding of the condition of being a PCSO. As neighbourhood policing was a nation-wide policing method in England and Wales at the time of the research, one group of PCSOs alone would limit the degree to which the social phenomenon of 'PCSO' could be understood in its various manifestations in a wide range of contexts (urban, rural, and suburban). This is not to suggest that the study conducted here was 'representative' of all PCSOs. This is not the goal of ethnography or of other qualitative research methods. Rather, this project is in keeping with the methodology of a *multisite ethnography*. First proposed by Marcus (1995), the multisite ethnography acknowledges that social phenomenon or even social groups are not always bounded by a designated space, and that moving with one's participants through space, as well as through time, can be integral to the ethnographic process (Falzon 2009). As Falzon argues, in the case of multisite ethnography, 'research design proceeds by a series of juxtapositions in which the global is collapsed into and made an integral part of parallel, related local situations, rather than something monolithic or external to them' (2009: 13). Hannerz (2003) echoes this when he writes that multisite ethnographies, 'draw on some problem, some formulation of a topic, which is significantly *trans*local, not to be confined within some single place' (2003: 206). In the case of the project discussed in this book, while each PCSO will have his or her own unique experiences in the role, the wider social and political forces affecting the working lives of PCSOs across England and Wales were also pertinent to their daily lives. Even changes to management practices of PCSOs in one force could have implications for those in another. Thus, moving beyond one NPT or one police force in an ethnographic method was needed to understand these occupational experiences fully.

To achieve this comprehensive understanding of the occupational experiences of PCSOs, multisite ethnographic observations were conducted in two northern English police forces. PCSOs from six NPTs (three teams from each force) were observed in the station and on patrol (foot, cycle, and occasionally in cars) for a total of 350 hours over a period of six months (October 2012 to March 2013). Field notes were taken to document the actors present, the events which occurred, and the observations made during these hours. Brief notes were made in the 'note' feature of my mobile phone as quickly as possible after a period of observation was completed, or during quiet moments in the police station or police car while the observation was ongoing. Mnemonic techniques were sometimes used to remember a series of events until an opportunity arose to note them down (Armstrong 1993; Reiner 2000). Upon return home, these notes would be transposed into a fuller, more detailed version in a Word document.

In addition to the observations, PCSOs and a selection of their police officer colleagues were also interviewed, using a combination of methods used by other police ethnographers such as Westmarland (2001) and by Hannerz (2003) in his multisite study of foreign news correspondents. Interviews generally took place in an office or quiet room in the police station, although one interview was conducted in a police car during a shift because of the time restrictions of the PCSO in question. PCSOs were asked to participate in an interview towards the end of their period of observation (more detail on this below). This was to allow a greater rapport to be built between the PCSOs and me, and for follow-up questions for events or comments made during the observations. Interviews lasted from 20 minutes to over an hour, and they were recorded so that they could be transcribed to a Word document later. Field notes and interview transcripts were then uploaded to MaxQDA (qualitative data analysis) software for coding and analysis.

The NPTs which I observed were chosen at random (using a stratified random sampling method) with a view to observing one urban, one suburban, and one rural area team from each police force (i.e. a variable sampling fraction, see Bryman 2001; Crow and Semmens 2008). Police force areas are generally subdivided into area units or 'neighbourhoods'. These area units were compiled into the three categories (urban, suburban, and rural) for each force, and a random number generator was used to select which neighbourhood area was observed from each category for that force. This was done to ensure exposure to a variety of neighbourhood policing conditions and contexts (see Cain 1971), and to prevent any existing knowledge I may have had about a particular area from influencing which neighbourhoods I chose to observe. Once permission to conduct the study had been granted from each police force, I met with the inspector responsible for each of the neighbourhoods I had selected from that force. The inspector and I discussed what would be the best way to select the PCSOs to invite to participate in the research. The inspector (or in some cases, the duty sergeant) would then inform their staff about the project, seek their agreement to participate, and then send me the names and contact details of the willing PCSOs to arrange observations. I made it as clear as I could to all police officers and staff involved that the study was voluntary and that they should not feel compelled to participate.[1] The choice of which PCSOs to invite to participate within those units was a combination of shift pattern, willingness to participate, and an effort to achieve a spread of age, experience, gender, and ethnicity. Once contact had been made with the PCSOs, I would discuss with them which days would be best to observe their work. In general, I observed each PCSO for one week, and each NPT for one month in total (about three or four PCSOs from each NPT over the course of the month). Selecting police constables or sergeants for interview was a less structured process (Hammersley and Atkinson 1995). Interviews with police officers were usually conducted towards the end of my time with a NPT so that the officers had seen me in the station for a few weeks and knew who I was. I would seek out officers who regularly worked with the PCSOs or the sergeants who supervised them and would arrange an interview time that suited their shift pattern.

Of the 21 PCSOs who were directly observed, seven were women, and three were from a minority ethnic group. From the 33 officers and staff who were interviewed, 15 were police constables (PCs) or sergeants, and 18 were PCSOs. Of the 15 police officers, three were women, and there were no ethnic-minority police officers interviewed. This was due to lack of black and minority ethnic police officers in the areas researched and the availability of officers for interview. Three of the observed PCSOs were not subsequently interviewed because of time restrictions or unavailability for interview. PCSOs and police officers quoted from the interviews and or mentioned in field notes in subsequent chapters

[1] However, as can be the case with ethnographies of the police, entirely voluntary participation may not have always been achieved because of adherence to the formal rank structure (O'Neill 2005).

are identified by the use of a pseudonym to ensure anonymity, along with his or her rank.

The Research Context

As policing and ethnographies are both context-specific activities, it is important to describe in detail the exact nature of the places and spaces in which this research took place. Each area had its own unique features, and challenges, and the officers and staff within them their own adaptations to these. The resulting occupational practices (both formal and informal) can only be fully understood through a comprehensive awareness of these contexts.

The first police force which was observed was a largely urban one, which I shall call the Northport Police Force.[2] Despite its large city-based population, there were also some small rural areas within its boundaries, as well as many suburban areas. The NPTs which were observed in Northport were based in Fallhill (a suburban, medium-sized community station), Marshton (an urban, large station with multiple policing teams present), and Starrybridge (a rural, small-sized community station). Each of these police stations and the teams within them will be described in turn, pointing out key features and the types of occupational relationships which were observed between the police officers and PCSOs.

Fallhill station was located in a middle-class suburb of the city in an old, traditional police building (late nineteenth century). It no longer had a functioning front desk for the public and, and the time of the research, was preparing to close down completely. The building was thus not fully staffed as would have been the case 10 years previously. Most of the officers and staff were located on the first floor, with lockers and equipment on the ground floor. There was one room on the ground floor dedicated for PCSOs to use, but the inspector had requested that all officers and staff work on the same floor (the first floor) for safety and team-building purposes. As such, most of the PCSOs and PCs shared a large, open-plan office with a small kitchen attached. The inspectors and sergeants used offices adjacent to the open-plan room. The ground floor also included the break room and a slightly larger kitchen, where officers and staff would eat their meals.

[2] As with the participant's names, all place names are also pseudonyms to protect anonymity.

PCs and PCSOs tended to mix in this station, both in the open-plan office and at meal times. Most shifts included about three PCSOs and three or four PCs, plus a sergeant and an inspector. In general, the officers and staff seemed to work together amicably. They had one briefing for the entire shift, which sometimes was led by a PCSO. There was friendly chatting among all NPT members during the shifts, and while PCs and PCSOs were 'paired' in terms of which areas they were to patrol, PCSOs tended to do this work on their own.

Marshton station was a new-build, large police station with multiple floors located in a densely populated, largely working-class residential area of the city. There was a functioning front desk, which was open to the public, and multiple teams, departments, and area units were based in the building. Several of these teams were once located in smaller, local police stations, which have since been closed down. During the time of the research, there was a degree of adjustment to the new arrangements still going on to the extent that the inspector did not know all of the PCSOs in the NPTs very well. Likewise, some of the PCSOs and PCs were still getting to know each other, and the tension this produced in the office was noticeable. The floor of the building which houses the NPTs had multiple offices within it, as well as a canteen, a large meeting room, and a prayer room. The PCs and PCSOs had use of two large open-plan offices, as well as one small additional office for the exclusive use of PCSOs. While all officers and staff were welcome to use the canteen for meal breaks, the PCSOs tended to take their meals out on their beat areas. This was partly due to logistics as it would take a great deal of time to travel back for meals, but was also partly due to wanting to have a quiet place to eat, sometimes with other PCSOs. There was not a great deal of integration of PCs and PCSOs in this station, although there were some notable exceptions to this. However, these successful collaborations between PCs and PCSOs seemed to be more the product of particular personalities, rather than the result of operational necessity or decisions by managers. It was difficult to determine exactly how many PCs and PCSOs were on each shift as there were multiple teams present at any one time, but it averaged about five PCSOs and six PCs on duty during the day, plus two sergeants and an inspector.

Starrybridge was a small community station located in a rural town, with regular public transport connections to a larger urban area nearby within the Northport Police Force. The team was located in a purpose-built building in the heart of the High Street, with about six PCSOs and four police officers on duty during the day. The building had three floors, two of which house the offices which PCSOs and PCs shared, while the subground level included staff lockers and a storage area. There was a large common room in the top floor with a kitchen, which both PCs and PCSOs used for their breaks and meal times. There was also a front desk which used to be open to the public but was closed at the time of the research for cost-saving purposes. In the main, the PCSOs and the PCs in this station worked very well together. Officers and staff would often attend calls together, and PCSOs were encouraged and supported in developing their own initiatives in the community (to address things like anti-social behaviour or to deter shoplifting). The team operated as a well-integrated unit, with each member having a specific and valued role to play. If an intervention was needed in an ongoing issue or incident in the community, the PCs and PCSOs would discuss together the course of action to take and freely share with each other the information they had about the event or suspects.

The Aldhamshire Police Force, the second police service to be observed, was a more mixed policing area in terms of having both densely populated urban spaces and large rural areas within its borders. The NPTs observed here were Hedgebourne (a suburban, large station with multiple police teams present), Wellspring (a rural, small community station), and Fayhaven (an urban, medium-sized community station). Each will be described in turn.

Hedgebourne was a large station in a suburban area which housed multiple policing teams and units. There was still a functioning front desk open to the public, and multiple NPTs were based there. The neighbourhood policing offices were located on one of the upper floors, with access to their own kitchen and large lounge and eating area. Most of the NPT officers and staff used a large open-plan office which had multiple computer terminals, as well as chargers for phones and radios. Team briefings also usually took place in this room, although officers often briefed themselves by reading through the daily information and intelligence on their own. The building also had a few meeting rooms with internal video conferencing facilities for briefings with officers and staff in other divisions of the police force. The inspector's office was adjacent to the open-plan office and the sergeants shared a smaller office nearby. The PCSOs and PCs tended to work together well and shared the open-plan office freely, often joking with and teasing each other. There was not much segregation of officers and staff, although the PCSOs did seem to work mainly with each other rather than with the PCs when out on patrol. A usual NPT shift would involve about three or four PCSOs, four PCs, one sergeant, and one inspector.

Wellspring was the smallest police station I observed, and it was located in a rural area not far from a large city. It was a very old building located on the high street of the village. The ground floor, which was mainly used by police officers, had a shared office, and a break room with a kitchen at one end. The PCSOs were based upstairs in two offices, but they shared the downstairs kitchen with the police officers. The PCs and the PCSOs did not integrate very much, partly because the local community officer was on long-term sick leave during my observations. The other PCs who used the station were mainly response officers, so it was difficult to get a sense of what the relationships were like within the station. There were normally two PCSOs on duty at any one time, but when shifts overlapped, this moved up to four. These PCSOs often worked in pairs. This is unusual practice for PCSOs as the concern is that members of the public may be deterred from approaching PCSOs who are in conversation with each other. However, because of the distances these PCSOs needed to travel to cover their large beat areas, it was felt to be safer if they did not work alone. The pairs of PCSOs worked well together and had been doing so for some time.

The last NPT I observed, based in Fayhaven, was housed in a very small station in a densely populated area of a large city in the Aldhamshire Police Force. Like the local area, the police station itself was also densely populated, with both PCs and PCSOs based there in close quarters. There was a large open-plan office which PCSOs and PCs shared, several smaller offices usually occupied by managers, and a small kitchen on the ground floor. The subground level housed the staff's lockers and the toilets. There was one conference room which also doubled as a break room during meal times. During the day, there were about seven PCSOs and about six to seven police officers on duty at any one time. The PCSOs and PCs here did not often work together. While relationships in the station were polite, the PCSOs usually worked separately from the PCs. There was not a great deal of open sharing of intelligence and communal planning of police work. The two groups largely operated independently of each other.

At the time of the research (late 2012 to early 2013), police forces in England and Wales were preparing for the impact of the Coalition Government's reduction in funding for policing (which would amount to a 20% cut over the course of 5 years), as well as the introduction of Police and Crime Commissioners (PCCs), due to come into post in early 2013. All PCSOs were acutely aware that this conflation of events could have serious consequences for the security of their employment. Police officers cannot be made redundant, but police staff, including PCSOs, can. At this point in time, it was unknown how the budget reductions would unfold in each force until the PCC had arrived. These issues are taken up in more detail in Chapter 7, but it is important to mention them here as these wider political events had a noticeable influence on relationships and conversations within the stations and between PCSOs. Some PCSOs felt more isolated at this time than had been the case previously, and this was demonstrated in their use of space in the stations and on their beats. It is precisely this manipulation of frontstage and backstage areas in the course of personal interactions that Goffman's dramaturgical framework analyses so well, and thus why it was chosen as a key theoretical framework for this book.

Goffman's Dramaturgy

Goffman's dramaturgical metaphor (which uses the image of the theatrical stage to describe social interaction) provides a useful analytical tool for examining the relationships between PCSOs and their police colleagues in the NPTs I observed. Manning (1977) utilized the dramaturgic metaphor for a detailed analysis of the symbolism of police work in the United States, and as this book will illustrate, its utility continues with the work and performances of PCSOs. Dramaturgy, as first discussed in *The Presentation of Self in Everyday Life* (1959), is one of Goffman's most well-known contributions to sociology, and it emerges in varying degrees of prominence throughout his work from the mid-1950s onwards (Smith 2013). According to Branaman (1997: xlv), 'Erving Goffman is the quintessential sociologist of everyday social life.' Instead of investigating the eventful and unusual aspects of existence, Goffman concerns himself primarily with the ways people keep direct encounters with others uneventful and orderly, organizing their interpersonal conduct to produce the 'interaction order' (Smith 2013: 58). By this Goffman is referring to the unwritten rules of social order, 'the structure of face-to-face interaction, and the nuances of the interaction process' (Birrell 1978: 16). Dramaturgy was his first and most influential method for doing this. As the routine and mundane is the context in which PCSOs most often encounter their police officer counterparts, a dramaturgical analysis of their interactions is warranted.

For Goffman, the self is utterly a social construct, with there being no one 'true' self, waiting for expression. Instead, Goffman argues that we juggle multiple selves and seek the best way to present the most applicable one in any situation (Smith 2013), based on the resources available and the likelihood of conveying a believable performance (Branaman 1997). In dramaturgy, Goffman uses the metaphor of the stage to describe this process. For him, we are actors on a stage when we engage in a face-to-face encounter with another person (our audience). We are at pains to present the best side of ourselves to this audience, and hide or rehearse those aspects which are weaker when we are out of sight of the audience. According to Goffman (1959), we employ a variety of tools to do this. He discusses these through the dramaturgical themes of 'performances' and 'teamwork', and the use of space, referred to as 'regions'. Goffman also examines threats to our performances and the techniques we use to prevent the performance from going wrong (such as tripping and falling or revealing we are not as adept at a task as we had implied). These threats are referred to as 'discrepant roles' and 'communication out of character', and the techniques employed to manage these are the 'arts of impression management' (Goffman 1959; Smith 2013). All of these have relevance for the PCSOs observed in police stations and on the beat when interacting with their police colleagues, and each theme will be described below.

The first theme within dramaturgy which Goffman describes is that of 'performances'. This refers to the steps we take to encourage our audiences to believe the character we are trying to embody during our interaction with them. According to Goffman (1959), in order to ensure that our performances are believable, that the interaction at hand runs smoothly and our audiences are comfortable with us and the situation, we carefully manage our performance 'front', which includes things such as the setting and our clothing, equipment, hair, bodily gestures, etc. Aspects of ourselves which are more difficult to control also feature as part of our 'front', such as sex, age, and ethnicity. Goffman argues that we regularly endeavour to present coherence between the setting, our appearance (how we look), and our manner (how we behave). He discusses the difficulties that actors have when they are taking up a new social role for which there is no established performance front. Many social roles are so well-established that they have become institutionalized with stereotypical expectations attached to them. The police could be seen in this regard, as those who encounter the police are likely to have certain expectations about what a police officer will do in particular situations. The social role of police officer has significance and stability that exists out with the specific actions a particular police officer may take. While PCSOs operate in very similar conditions to the police officers and with a similar performance front, they do not completely fit the police officer template. They cannot arrest, they cannot use force, and they have differences in their uniform. As a relatively new social role, building a performance front which is regarded in its own right as legitimate and competent has been on ongoing challenge for PCSOs, and later chapters will discuss this in more detail.

Goffman's second theme is 'teamwork'. He proposes that while it appears that anyone engaged in a performance does so alone, it is actually the case that performers operate as individual members of a larger performance unit. Even if there are no other members of that unit present, the standards and moral guidelines for that group will dictate the interaction of the performer. These standards generally stem from a reference group of some kind, such as an occupational or social role, with whom the performer identifies. Goffman (1959) refers to any group of people who collaborate in staging the same performance (presenting the same *definition of the situation*) as a 'performance team', or just a 'team'. He argues that '(w)hether the members of a team stage similar individual performances or stage dissimilar performances which fit together into a whole, an emergent team impression arises which can conveniently be treated as a fact in its own right […]' (1990: 85). There are two key components of performance teams for Goffman. The first is that as all members of the team are dependent upon each other for the success of the performance, and, therefore, one member can spoil the performance for the others if he or she does not maintain the expected standards. The other element is that performance teammates have a degree of informality between them, which means that when outsiders are not present, the performance can be suspended. It will be demonstrated in later chapters how the PCSO performance teams I observed operated, who their audiences were, how they maintained performance standards among their group, and how their performances changed when these audiences were absent.

Goffman (1959) has discussed the use of space in detail, in what comprises his third dramaturgical theme of 'regions', and what it reveals about performance teams. He refers to the area where performances are delivered for an audience as the 'front region' and the areas where performances (including one's appearance) are rehearsed or contradicted as the 'back region' or 'backstage'. Generally, audience members are restricted to front regions (or the 'frontstage') so that they are not able to see behaviour from a performance team which might contradict the definition of the situation that team is trying to project (Goffman 1959). Back regions are also usually the places where a performance team will relax and speak to each other in a more informal way than they would do in front of audience members. Goffman notes that as it is vital to the success of any interaction performance that the audience does not gain access to the backstage region, this area is usually physically separate or cut off from the front region in some way, but is also close enough for the performers to access when they need support or a chance to relax. As will be demonstrated in later chapters, PCSOs did have their own backstage areas, but these were much more difficult to control or to preserve as separate spaces due to the physical constraints of police stations and the other areas in which they would meet. However, these officers were adept at finding ways around these restrictions to maintain some degree of segregated space for their performance team to rehearse performances, to correct the performances of wayward teammates, and to relax. These proved to be vital coping mechanisms for those performance teams which were regularly challenged as to the legitimacy of their definition of the situation.

After considering how social interaction between performance teams is intended to work, Goffman (1959) then turns his attention to the ways in which performances can go wrong and to what is done to try to prevent or mitigate these errors. The first aspect he considers is that of 'discrepant roles'. These are individuals who have knowledge of a team's secrets or other types of destructive information that could prove fatal to the impression the team or performer is trying to convey should this information become more widely known. Goffman describes a wide variety of discrepant roles (such as the informer, the shill, the spotter, the mediator, etc.), but there is one which is of particular significance for the current study: that of 'the colleague'. According to Goffman, the colleague stages a similar performance and routine to similar audiences, but does not participate as a teammate with the performance team in question. Colleagues 'share a community of fate' (Goffman 1990: 159) with our performance team in that they have experienced similar difficulties in staging the performance, share a similar point of view and also share a social language. Therefore, they cannot completely hide all their performance secrets from each other in the way that they hide them from the audience. This then means of course that colleagues have the ability to spoil each other's performances as they have access to this discrediting information. As they are not full teammates, a spoiled performance for one performance team does not necessarily spoil the performance of their colleagues. This is the type of relationship which emerged between PCSOs and their police officer colleagues. PCSOs and PCs do not operate as teammates, as the following research will demonstrate, but they do work in similar contexts, with similar audiences and with similar performance fronts. They therefore have discrediting information about each other but because of their differentiated claims to power and authority, police constables did not need to fear that a discredited PCSO performance would reflect badly on the definition of the situation which they (as constables) were attempting to convey. This intimate yet imbalanced relationship resulted in, at times, strained encounters between PCs and PCSOs.

'Communication out of character' is another of Goffman's (1959) analyses into deviations from standard interaction performances. In this case, the performers knowingly behave in ways that are outside of the usual 'script' for their team. This can involve using a secret language or cues to communicate with teammates while still in the presence of the audience, but these are usually done in such a way as to not spoil the overall performance. The PCSOs I observed in the less well-integrated neighbourhood teams would on occasion do this in the presence of PCs or supervisors, for example, by exchanging knowing looks across the open-plan office. However, there were also times when PCSOs and PCs would be united in their communication out of character in the presence of a more senior officer (van Hulst 2017). Goffman refers to this as 'realigning actions' which can be done between two groups of different status who temporarily collude with one another. These actions are used to bring these usually separate and oftentimes competitive teams together in the presence of a common audience. There were moments during my observations where the officers and staff shared inside knowledge which they did not want to reveal to their common supervisor, and during these moments, realigning actions were evident. This included sharing knowing smiles during the supervisor's rant about something in the office that was not to his liking, or deliberate collusion to conceal an infraction by one of the team members from the supervisor. However, these moments of collusion were usually temporary and only served to reinforce the usual division that existed between the PCs and the PCSOs as separate performance teams, especially in the neighbourhood units, which were less well-integrated in their work.

The final group of performance techniques to control performances which Goffman (1959) discusses is 'the arts of impression management'. Some of these behaviours include the techniques used by audiences to ensure that they do not interfere with a team's performance, such as by deliberately avoiding backstage areas or being inattentive to conversation between teammates. What are of more relevance for the current study are the techniques used by teammates to ensure the best possible performance is given at any time. These include dramaturgical *loyalty, discipline*, and *circumspection*. Loyalty to one's performance team can be encouraged by presenting the audience as inhuman or 'other' in some way. This is not unusual for police officers to do (Holdaway 1983), and it was apparent among PCSOs in this research project. By having a common audience, a complete 'social community' can be fostered between teammates and between colleagues, as was often the case for PCSOs and PCs, especially in the more integrated neighbourhood teams. They would offer each other moral support in the face of a common audience—the local public. Police officers and staff are also accustomed to dramaturgical discipline, which refers to the practice of controlling one's face, voice, and overall reactions to events as they unfold. PCs and PCSOs can face unexpected circumstances and events during the course of their work and must retain a professional appearance and manner, as was apparent throughout my observations (Manning 1977). The final element of impression management which Goffman (1959) discusses is that of dramaturgical circumspection. It is here where PCSOs have less control of crafting their impressions than may be the case for other performance groups. This refers to the way in which performance teams select, as best they can, the members of their team and the conditions in which they perform in order to foster the best impression possible. PCSOs have little influence in the selection of those with whom they work, where they will work, and who the audience will be. However, there were occasions where PCSOs could prepare for a performance, for example, when giving a presentation to a community safety group or a school visit, and on these occasions, they may enlist the help of a PC in their preparations or in the performance itself to ensure it has as much credibility as possible.

While Goffman's (1959) dramaturgy is indeed a useful theoretical framework to employ to understand the personal interactions I observed during the ethnography, larger institutional-level processes and decisions also had a bearing on the experiences of PCSOs (which they discussed with me in the interviews). These and their effect on PCSOs will be examined in Chapter 4, where dramaturgy will have less of a bearing on the analysis. However, the macro- and microlevel analyses will be brought back together in the final part of the book, as both did clearly inform each other and both will contribute to the resulting occupational culture of PCSOs.

Conclusion

This chapter has considered the research methods, research contexts, and theoretical framing employed in the study of PCSOs on which this book is based. The primary research method was a multisite ethnography, which included participant observation and in-depth interviewing. Six neighbourhood areas and their respective NPTs were observed from two different police forces in the north of England over a period of six months. These areas represent a variety of policing contexts, from low-income inner-city areas to more remote and affluent rural areas. A key method of analysis for the resultant research findings was Goffman's dramaturgical metaphor. As it is a technique for understanding the symbolic meanings which stem from personal interaction and gestures, a dramaturgical perspective complements well ethnographic data collection.

What this study and the resulting analysis have revealed is an occupational environment in which PCSOs and their police officer colleagues engage in daily rituals which confirm or challenge, to varying degrees, the place of PCSOs as legitimate members of the policing organization. In those neighbourhood teams where PCSOs were largely accepted as having an important contribution to the success of neighbourhood policing, interactions tended to reflect this through dramaturgical arrangements such as integrated backstage areas for PCs and PCSOs, a lack of open challenges to PCSO decisions in front of members of the public, and team-building conversations which presented the public as a mutually difficult outside group. In the neighbourhood teams where PCSOs are not as easily accepted as legitimate policing actors, this was clearly discerned in aspects of their dramaturgical performances, such as backstage areas that are segregated between PCs and PCSOs, PCSOs regularly seizing opportunities to visibly demonstrate their worth to PC colleagues, and a lack of moral support for PCSOs' performances in front of members of the public. However, all PCSO groups, even those in the more integrated neighbourhood teams, faced a daily routine of consciously monitoring their performances and impression management, as any slight infraction would have significant consequences for the performance of PCSOs generally, although this risk was greater in some teams more than in others. This stems from a larger systematic institutional process of undermining the role of PCSO which commenced with the arrival of the first cohort of PCSOs in the early 2000s and continues to this day. Strategic decisions such as short training periods, lack of refresher training, and little professional development for PCSOs sent messages from management levels about the worth of PCSOs for the organization as a whole, and those messages find expression in personal interactions within NPTs.

The chapters to follow in this book will explore these processes in more detail, considering a variety of experiences, interactions, and audiences extracted from the ethnography of PCSOs reported here. It will begin in Part II, where Chapter 3 discusses the primary activities in which PCSOs engaged during my time with them. This will consider a 'typical' day for a PCSO, as well as engagement, enforcement, administrative, and emergency-response tasks. It will also examine the skills PCSOs feel they need to do their jobs well. Chapter 3 thus presents the ideal *definition of the situation* for PCSOs which they endeavour to perform when working in the public or when in the presence of police officer colleagues. Chapter 4 is an examination of the journey to becoming a PCSO in England, which not only includes the training involved but also the processes of learning the less formalized methods by which PCSOs do their work and learn their place in the organization. In Chapter 5, the book then moves to a consideration of how policing 'family' is experienced and how it functions in a pluralized public sector, including how this is demonstrated through the symbolic interactions of PCSOs and their police officer colleagues. By doing so, these three chapters will build a detailed picture of pluralized policing in England from the perspective of those within it. The final section of the book, Part III, will then consider whether a PCSO occupational culture can be identified (Chapter 6) and what these processes mean for community policing, especially in light of ongoing measures of fiscal restraint (Chapter 7).

PART II

The Police Community Support Officer

3

What Do Police Community Support Officers Do?

This chapter presents a detailed account of what Police Community Support Officers (PCSOs) do in their daily work, and the skills seen as essential in these tasks. This examination begins with a discussion of a 'typical' day for a PCSO in terms of its overall structure. It will then consider the types of activities in which PCSOs engaged during the course of the research. This will include crime control or enforcement-related tasks, community engagement tasks, administrative tasks, and, finally, emergency-related work. The chapter then moves to a discussion of the skills which were felt to be the most important for PCSOs to master: communication and the development of local knowledge. These analyses are important to consider first as they identify the ideal PCSO performance, the *definition of the situation* (Goffman 1959), which PCSOs will learn (as will be explored in Chapter 4) upon joining the organization and present and defend (in Chapter 5) to their police officer colleagues and to the community members with whom they interact. This discussion will utilize observations and interviews from the staff and officers of the six neighbourhood policing teams (NPTs) who participated in this study: Fallhill, Marshton, and Starrybridge from the Northport Police Force, and Hedgebourne, Wellspring, and Fayhaven from the Aldhamshire Police Force.

A Day in the Life

Although the daily experiences for any PCSO can be quite variable, there were some common elements to their routines across the NPTs. This section will explore these, as well as some of the local variations which were observed. Just like police constables, PCSOs start their shift by arriving at their police station to sign in, attend a briefing, get their assignments for the day, check e-mail, and gather their equipment. PCSO Deborah describes well a 'normal' day for her:

MO: What sorts of things do you do in your job, what's a typical day like?
Generally we come on duty […] and we have our briefing, and we research for our briefing. And then after that we will check our emails. Personally I like to research my intelligence of what's going on in my area so I know that I'm going out and I know what's going on. […] I also like to look at who's wanted and who's been arrested and for what reason. And that's also for my own safety so I know if it's kicked off with someone, to be a bit wary of speaking to that person in the future. So all that I think is really important and also we look at the community reports that tells you what's going on because all the PCSOs and PCs [on this beat] update that with they're up to and what they're doing, so that's good because its continuity. Then you'll go out and sometimes you're given your tasks from your emails and they can be from supervision, beat officers, inspectors. […] You make plans but sometimes you have to put them on hold because there are more pressing things to do. […] I've still got to put some more intelligence on, that's quite lengthy, so sometimes you don't get time to do that. Obviously intelligence should go on quite quickly but sometimes you don't have time to do it in that day if you've got other things that are a little bit more urgent. So you've got to weigh up what's more important than the other. […] Or ask one of your colleagues if they can do it for you because you work as a team so it's not a big problem. […] We do some patrolling obviously. Even when we are going to jobs and we are going to do tasks, you're still out on your beat and you're still there, so that's good. And obviously if you come across anything, you have to deal with it as and when. And you get sent to jobs by Comms [central communications] as well, obviously I got sent to that job but it was nice that Steve (a PCSO) said 'no I'll go to that because I'm round the corner'. So it's just team work, it's nice. (PCSO Deborah, Marshton)

PCSOs usually work alone in their beat areas (there were exceptions to this, which will be explored below) in order to make them more approachable and to encourage conversation with the public. As Deborah indicates, however, they will still support each other in their daily tasks when they can. All officers and staff on a particular shift will start their work at the same time and so tend to know each other well. PCSOs are meant to spend about 80% of their time outside of the police station so that they are 'visible' to the public. This means that the time spent in the station with the daily briefing and the initial preparations for their day and the time at the end to input intelligence into the database can be compressed. Some supervisors were stricter about this than others were. For example, one PCSO I interviewed mentioned an occasion where their inspector directed them to do an envelope-stuffing job outside in a public place so that they would still be visible to the community. In order to be able to support each other throughout the day, PCSOs must therefore be able to communicate with each other directly. This happens either through the official communication channels or more informally through their personal mobile phones.

In addition to the tasks Deborah mentioned above, some PCSOs who are on the first shift of the day will endeavour to attend their local school during drop-off and pick-up times. There are various reasons for this. In relation to primary schools, it is usually with a view to preventing parents from committing illegal or dangerous parking around the school, and to ensure children cross roads safely. The PCSOs will then sometimes go into the school briefly to greet the management or office staff and see if they are needed to speak to any of the classes. These presentations could be about various personal safety or crime prevention issues, such as not talking to strangers or not leaving empty boxes from Christmas presents on display outside next to bins (which would advertise what was inside that might be worth stealing). For secondary schools, visits usually happen after school to prevent anti-social behaviour (ASB) in the local area as the pupils make their way home. Thus there is a shift in focus here from children as potential victims of crime in primary schools to children being perpetrators of crime or ASB in secondary schools. This will be taken up again later in the chapter.

PCSOs use a variety of methods of transportation to get to and patrol their beat area, depending on the local topography, the weather, and the resources available to them (Merritt and Dingwall 2010). Generally speaking, PCSOs are not permitted to use police cars as a method of patrolling, in order to ensure that they can be available to and engage with the public in direct, face-to-face ways as much as possible. PCSOs in urban areas with extensive and reliable public transportation tend to use this method to get to their beats if those areas are not in walking distance. They then patrol on foot during their shift. Those PCSOs based in suburban locations where public transport is perhaps not as frequent often cycle to their beat areas. The question then arises as to whether they patrol on the bicycle and at what speed or park the bike somewhere safe and patrol on foot. To an extent this can be determined by how large an area they have to patrol or what they are planning to do on their beat that day. While patrolling on a bicycle is permitted, there was some debate among the research participants as to whether this allows for public engagement. See for example the following field notes:

PCSO Ellie doesn't think patrolling on bikes is a good idea. People won't stop you to chat or report a problem if you are on a bike. There is less interaction with the community on bikes. (Field note 9/10, Fallhill)

PCSO Charlie says that foot patrol is limiting - he can only cover about a quarter of the ground that he covers on his bike. He is always 'in the wrong place' on foot. Sometimes he is in the right place when a call comes in, but not often. (Field note 11/12, Starrybridge)

PCSO Tom cycles at a slow pace. He says that there is no point in rushing round as he would cover ground too fast, and there is too much time to kill. It is also hard for people to stop him for a chat if he is whizzing past. (Field note 16/12, Starrybridge)

PCSOs who are based in rural locations have particular transportation issues (Merritt and Dingwal 2010). They are less likely to have access to public transportation or to have the right conditions for cycling. In addition, their beats can be located some distance away from their police station. PCSOs in these situations will often arrange for the local community police officers to give them a lift to their beats and to collect them again later on. One rural area, Wellspring, not only permitted the PCSOs to travel and patrol in police cars (marked and unmarked), but also to conduct their work in pairs. The PCSOs in question felt they had strong grounds for this arrangement in that their beat areas were not only very remote and difficult to access, but if something should happen to them while on patrol, they would be safer with a colleague alongside. The pairs would patrol both beat areas over the course of the shift, and make a point of calling into community contact points such as the local shop or schools. The following field note indicates the justification the PCSOs have for using cars:

The PCSOs are struggling over the lack of available cars. This is not a problem if your patch is just outside the door, they argue. This is not the case here. It is a huge area and the other PCSO needs to go out to the sticks and needs to have a car. They have cars allocated to their team, but there isn't always enough of them. (Field note 7/02, Wellspring)

While this arrangement had existed for some time and had survived many attempts to challenge it (from management and PCSOs from other teams), towards the end of my observations, it was becoming clear that an impending removal of one of the patrol cars from the station and an increase in police officers based there would mean an end to the practice of PCSOs driving on patrol. It was unclear how they would manage their transportation in the future once this occurred. One PCSO, however, was not upset at this news:

> I'm almost disappointed with myself because we seem to have had more and more access to a vehicle and we use the vehicle. Now for me, my job is people seeing me in the street and talking to me, and because we have had jobs to go to that are maybe four or five miles away, we have used the car instead of walking. What I used to do is walk up [there], walk through the centre, talking to people, calling in different shops, talking to them on the way to an incident, and then I'd obviously attend the incident. [...] So that's something I'm conscious about and something that's probably going to change because my boss says that we are going to lose a car or not getting a car as often which I don't mind. I think it's important to be seen in the community on foot. (PCSO Neive, Wellspring)

A final dilemma that many PCSOs face each day is where to take meal breaks. For the urban PCSOs (or rural PCSOs in cars), it was usually not difficult to return to the police station, and they would often meet other PCSOs, or in some stations the PCs, there to have their meals together (this is discussed in detail in Chapter 5). These meetings were usually prearranged or agreed during the course of the shift. Suburban and rural PCSOs found it more difficult to do this, especially if their beat was at a distance from the station. In these cases, they would take their meals with them on patrol. There was a variety of locations where they would have their breaks. Some PCSOs made use of 'closed' police stations. These were properties which no longer had reception areas open to the public, but which the police force still owned and the officers and staff could access when needed for shelter or toilet breaks. In some areas, the PCSOs had access to properties (unoccupied council flats or small offices) which were co-owned with the local authority and in which they could go for breaks or to hold meetings with their public sector partners. Finally, there were several occasions where PCSOs took their breaks or meals in the staff break rooms of supermarkets or other businesses. This was seen as a type of community engagement in that they were making contact with the staff of local establishments who, I was told, liked to have them on the premises for crime prevention purposes.

Near the end of their shift, PCSOs will return to the main police station where they are based, usually by the same method of transportation that they used at the start of the shift. They would usually leave time before the scheduled end of their day to update databases (for example, if they had collected possible 'intelligence'), check e-mail, and do general administrative work. If their shift overlaps with the start of the next shift, they may give their recently arrived colleagues a verbal update on what happened in the beat that day. The PCSOs will then return their radios, change into civilian clothes, and go home. Unless there was a compelling reason to do so, PCSOs did not tend to stay on longer than their scheduled shift time, although this varied by NPT (as will be discussed further in Chapter 5).

PCSO Activities

As with police officers, PCSOs are engaged in a variety of tasks, and they have a wide range of responsibilities when out in public. Although the role of PCSO is intended to be a non-confrontational one and primarily focused on community engagement (Home Office 2001; ACPO 2007), this was far from the case during the course of the ethnography. This reflects Ranasinghe's (2017) argument about the difficulty in separating law-enforcement and community work in patrol-based policing, to the extent that he has challenged the degree to which the 'classic' police ethnographies from the 1960s onwards show a minimal amount of crime work is involved in police patrol. As the example above of school patrol demonstrated, while PCSOs were ostensibly present to protect primary school children from harm, this might be achieved by remonstrating with their law-breaking parents. More recently, Merritt (2010) has argued that the PCSO role is best viewed as occupying a continuum from enforcement to engagement tasks, with staff positioning themselves at various points along this line. Thus while the discussion below has separated enforcement work from community engagement for the purposes of presentational simplicity, it is acknowledged that this is at times a difficult distinction to make, and some overlap between the categories will be apparent. Activities related to administration work and emergencies will also be considered in this section.

Enforcement

There were many tasks and roles which PCSOs performed that were related to crime control. This ranged from those which supported police officers in their investigations of local crimes and did not involve direct engagement with the public to tasks that are more confrontational, such as detaining suspects or issuing fixed penalty notices. These will be discussed in turn, beginning with the less confrontational roles. In terms of supporting PCs in their investigations, PCSOs are often asked to gather copies of CCTV footage from shops where a theft had occurred or to take evidence from a crime to a larger station for storage. As an example of the latter, there was one rather memorable occasion where I found myself in a police car with two PCSOs and about £15,000 worth of cannabis in several large plastic bags. (Even with the windows down, we were all a bit lightheaded by the time we arrived at the other station where the evidence was to be stored.) While these tasks may seem mundane and routine, if they are not performed correctly there can be consequences for the PCSO involved as PCSO Dave discovered:

Dave had his first CCTV evidence report earlier in the month rejected because there was not enough detail of the offender and time of the event. He is really annoyed - he felt it was not his job to get into issues of description. That is the job of the imaging department. [...] The sergeant didn't look into the reasons behind the rejection - he just passed it back to Dave. So rather than retrieving the original disc in the police stores (which would involve a trip to the larger area station and be more paperwork), he went to the shop in question to see the footage on screen. He doesn't like all these little jobs, he would rather be out patrolling; doing what his job is meant to do. He doesn't like being in the station filling out forms. (Field note 17/10, Fallhill)

Some PCSOs who I observed were able to write their own statements when they were witnesses to a crime or to take reports for 'negative lines' crimes. The latter refers to an event where there is no possibility of finding the culprit because of a lack of evidence (no further lines of enquiry). Both of these tasks required a degree of additional training and were skills that PCSOs found improved the more they did them. However, as these were not events that happened very often, they could easily make mistakes on the forms, which PCs would then need to correct. This was especially important for witness statements, which PCSOs can also take for certain crimes. They will speak to the person affected by the crime, as well as to the people in the adjacent properties when appropriate. This door-to-door work is something that PCSOs are often asked to do in order to save time for police officers to allow them to work on the more serious offences. PCSO Charlie describes some of these tasks during our interview:

> You can be putting crime submissions in, theft from motor vehicles, burglary to sheds that aren't attached to dwellings, we can't put burglaries in. We have got a list of crimes that we can put in and we can't put in. When I say putting a crime in, I mean we record all the details off the victim, so we take the time it's happened to and from, we take all the victims details, what they work as, their contact details so that we can contact them. […] There might be a point where it comes to light that CCTV is on the street or something like that when you're taking the crime, so then you would have to go and get the CCTV. You would have to conduct house to house enquiries on the street, and speak to the neighbours whereby you might come across a neighbour that's seen something. So you then take a witness first account off the neighbour stating what they've seen in your pocket notebook. I only did that a couple of weeks ago and we made enquiries after that, so then it would go to a police officer to investigate it. (PCSO Charlie, Starrybridge)

As Charlie describes, PCSOs will do a degree of investigation for these crimes, with gathering statements and chasing any potential CCTV footage of the event. Should it emerge that there is some evidence of who the offender might be (a line of enquiry), the case will then be passed to a PC to complete. PCs described to me in interviews how some PCSOs know local people better than the PC does and can at times identify suspects from CCTV footage or descriptions from witnesses, which assists the PC in making an arrest.

While PCSOs often do 'jobs', such as those above, which directly assist a police officer or save officers some administrative work, patrol is a large part of the day for a PCSO, and it is often within this context that the other enforcement tasks are performed. While being visible and accessible to the community is an important aspect of patrol (more on this below), there are elements of patrol which are more aligned to crime work and crime prevention. For example, 'hot spot' patrolling was used in both the Aldhamshire Police Force and the Northport Police Force. The idea is to focus police or PCSO presence in certain areas which have been identified as likely places for crime to occur at certain times of the day. Central analytical services are to conduct this predictive analysis and to inform local areas of when and where the hot spots are. This is based on academic research, such as that by Weisburd et al (2012), which indicates that patrols which are carefully targeted can be more effective at crime prevention than random patrols are. However, the detail of the hot spot method did not seem to have completely transferred into practice here. In theory, 'hot spots' are 'microlocations', such as a specific street corner, which are patrolled for about 15 to 20 minutes. The following field note describes how the PCSOs were instructed to do them in one NPT:

Hot spots are identified by analysts based on recent crimes recorded in their area and are communicated to the NPTs during the daily briefing. Hot spot patrolling takes PCSOs away from their usual area and they may not see their contacts for a while. They have to cancel appointments that they might have had. It used to be that staff were just advised to keep eye out on a hot spot. Now supervisors assign a PCSO or two to the area and the local tracking system is checked to see if they are there. If a beat officer (PC) isn't on duty they will pull PCSOs off other beats to do the patrols. The PCs or PCSOs have to be walking or cycling around the area the entire time, and the time period is usually for a couple hours. The geographical radius can be rather small – the distance of three or four city blocks. It gets tedious and PCSO Gary says it is a matter of shutting the barn door after the horse has bolted. Hot spots are decided by crime analysts after an incident has happened, with high and medium priority areas, with circles on a map near where the crime was as the hot spot radius. Maps are sent out in daily briefings and PCSOs must be in those zones during a pre-determined window of time. If it falls overnight, PCSOs can't do it as their shifts end at 10pm. (Field note 4/10, Fallhill)

In this example, the hot spot is larger than one street junction, and it is patrolled for more than an hour, forcing PCSOs to cancel plans for the day and often to be away from their usual beat areas for extended periods. Another intensive patrol method which PCSOs can be asked to do are local 'days of action'. These are used where a particular area is identified as having a recurring crime problem. PCSOs and PCs will 'flood' the area with patrols, sometimes also with a mobile police unit parked nearby, and will go door to door issuing crime prevention advice. This again takes PCSOs away from their usual areas and activities for large periods of time (Cosgrove and Ramshaw 2013).

When PCSOs are not engaged in focused or directed patrols, they will usually decide for themselves how to patrol their beat area, taking into account any 'jobs' they have planned or meetings they had scheduled, and will design their routes accordingly. While patrolling, PCSOs will be looking for suspicious activity or people. By having a usual beat that they patrol often, PCSOs feel they are more aware of activity that seems out of place, a technique not unlike that used by police officers (Sacks 1972; Loftus 2009; Reiner 2010). They will also look out for people who are wanted or for missing cars that they were informed about in the daily briefing. When something or someone attracts their attention, they will make of note of it and, if appropriate, input the event to the intelligence database when they return to the station, as the following field note describes:

The PCSOs put intelligence reports into the system when they see someone they recognise who is 'known' to the police, even if they see that person just in passing, especially if the person is one of their known offenders. That way if a crime happens nearby there is a record of that person being there. (Field note 8/11, Marshton)

If PCSOs have conversations with members of the public who give them information that might be considered intelligence, this will also go on the database. PCSOs often refer to themselves as the 'eyes and ears' of the police. While they cannot always act on the information themselves, they feel they are more likely to be able to collect this information through the relationships they have built in their communities and their familiarity with the area that local PCs might not have. PCSO Chris feels this is an important aspect of the PCSO role that benefits a variety of teams:

Since we have moved to [this large area station] and we are easily accessible by the CID [the detectives] and the duty group officers, it's a lot easier to exchange information regarding different jobs that different officers are dealing with, and gaining a successful conclusion to any incidents. We can help them, they can help us. […] A PCSO I think should know the area he/her is responsible for. And when you've been working an area for a certain length of time, people do get to know you and they will feel comfortable in talking to you about certain things which you can pass on, intelligence reports etc., and it's all to make the job easier and get detections of crime. (PCSO Chris, Hedgebourne)

As part of their usual patrols, PCSOs can be tasked with checking on known offenders who are required to be in their homes at certain times of the day as part of their community sentence or probation. Not all offenders at home have electronic tags; some are just issued with curfews. The offenders are graded according to the seriousness of their offence. Those who are the more serious offenders are checked about twice a day, and the less serious ones about once a week. The PCSOs did not enjoy this job. While the offenders themselves were usually polite at the door, family and friends could become very annoyed at the regular intrusions. This is an example of how a task which seems on the surface to be non-confrontational can easily escalate into one that has a real risk of confrontation for the PCSO. Although the PCSO role was created with the intention of it being non-confrontational, this seems to be an inherent element of the job. As PCSO Alfie notes, at times it is not possible for PCSOs to avoid confrontation:

They say that this is not a confrontational role, and for some areas it won't be, but for areas like this, it is, there's absolutely no denying that. The depth of anti-police feeling from a hell of a lot of people around these areas is phenomenal. As soon as you put on this uniform, as soon as you do that job, effectively we are telling people not to do what they want to do, so inevitably that's going to upset them. And doing this role, it will generate quite a lot of ill feeling so naturally that will manifest itself in some sort of physical confrontation and some people deal better with that than others. (PCSO Alfie, Fayhaven)

There are other enforcement-related tasks for PCSOs which carry the risk of confrontation or are by their nature confrontational. The first example of an enforcement-related task which can be confrontational for PCSOs is issuing fixed penalty notices for certain types of ASB. For the Aldhamshire and Northport Police Forces, these could be issued for low-level offences such as cars causing an obstruction, expired tax discs (when these were issued on paper), cycling on the pavement, dog fouling, littering, and 'anti-social use of a motor vehicle'. PCSOs are not allowed to stop cars which are in motion or to issue tickets for drivers who are 'wilfully' causing an obstruction (i.e. drivers who refuse to move their vehicle when asked) as these are considered confrontations. However, even when PCSOs were within their power to issue a ticket, they tended to warn people first and ask them to stop what they were doing in order to avoid a negative reaction. Some even reported that they preferred to issue tickets only when they were working with another PCSO or a PC. This suggests that the few fixed penalty notices which they are allowed to issue are in themselves confrontational events.

The PCSOs in this study also had the ability to initiate restorative justice processes if they felt it would lead to better outcome than would issuing a fixed penalty notice or commencing procedures for an ASB order. 'Restorative justice' refers to a process whereby victim and offender come together in a mediated meeting to discuss the event in question and to find a resolution of some kind. There is training available to PCSOs for restorative justice, but only up to a certain level. PCSOs can do immediate restorative justice between two people when an event has just happened, or they can arrange a group restorative justice meeting at a later date (Levels 1 and 2, see ACPO 2011). Restorative justice seemed to be used primarily with children and young people in order to avoid starting them down a criminal justice path with the use of interventions that are more formal. There were also examples of PCSOs arranging restorative justice meetings with adults, such as to resolve neighbour disputes or to deal with a repeat shoplifter. There were times, however, when the PCSOs questioned how effective this method was or felt that it was merely a way of resolving matters quickly without the need for additional paperwork. For example, the following field note was taken when observing PCSO Steve:

One kid on Steve's beat stole his Nan's car and smashed it. It was resolved through restorative justice (RJ), but as it was his Nan the RJ experience didn't have a big impact. Steve feels the kid saw it as getting away with it with no punishment. (Field note 26/11, Marshton)

In addition to issuing fixed penalty notices and arranging restorative justice interventions, the PCSOs in this study also had the power to stop a member of the public and take note of their details, a 'stop and account'. This is also a confrontational task, even without the power to search the individual. As PCSO Gary describes, there are various reasons for why a PCSO would stop a member of the public:

Like I say, we are out there to be the eyes and the ears and see what's going on, so really if it's just somebody walking down the street, there's

> no reason whatsoever to stop them. But if we are on the [hot spot] areas, like we have been yesterday and today, and if you look back at what's happened in the previous couple of days for that area, there might have been a robbery, there might have been a burglary, there might have been a description put out of somebody that was in that area. So you might see somebody that matches that description, you might see somebody who's carrying a bag ... A lot of it's a gut feeling really, and you think maybe there's something going on. Sometimes you might talk to them and everything's completely above board, so no harm done, it's just one of those things. (PCSO Gary, Fallhill)

This relates to the earlier discussion of PCSOs gathering intelligence in their beat areas for wider use among the policing teams. Every stop and account must be registered with the database to track how often these are done, with whom as well as the person's demographic information and the reason for the stop. If there is no justifiable reason a stop cannot take place, the PCSOs can register the sighting in their notebook instead and log it in the intelligence database later. During the course of the ethnography, Aldhamshire Police Force phased in the power of search for PCSOs. As with stop and accounts, a stop and search needs to be based on reasonable suspicion. I witnessed one PCSO do a stop and search, and this was with a young person who the PCSO had seen throw a snowball at a car and who then subsequently lied about his name and address. PCSO Neive (Wellspring) said that the power of search gives the PCSOs more teeth, and it means that they do not need to wait for a PC to come and do it.

The final element of confrontational enforcement-related work which PCSOs do is that of detaining someone for up to 30 minutes while they wait for a police officer to come to conduct an arrest. PCSOs are not warranted officers and so are not able to arrest members of the public in the way that PCs can. They do, however, have the power of citizen's arrest (as does anyone) but have been discouraged from using this as it could confuse members of the public, as well as the PCSOs themselves, as to where the boundary is between them and police officers. It could also potentially open the doors to litigation against the PCSO if the arrest was not performed appropriately. I did observe one occasion where a PCSO detained a suspect while waiting on a police officer to arrive. PCSO Charlie (Starrybridge) needed to detain the same suspect twice in the course of about 20 minutes because initially she was reported as only being 'a suspicious person' and then later was reported as wanted for burglary. On the first occasion, he took her details and managed to stall her through conversation until these were checked by Communications (for outstanding warrants—which at that point had not yet registered on the system for this individual). In the second encounter, he needed to stall her again until a police officer arrived to arrest her and again managed it through conversation. He told her there had been an issue with her record and that a police officer was coming to ask her a few questions. This of course was not the full truth but was enough to keep her from trying to leave. Neither of these encounters was easy to do, and both showed the skill required of a PCSO to maintain the non-confrontational nature of the role. This reflects one of Cosgrove's (2015) three PCSO typologies, that of the 'Professional' PCSO. These are PCSOs who are able to balance the enforcement and engagement aspects of the role and thus show an adeptness at their craft.

Many PCSOs I interviewed and observed discussed the range of powers that they have. PCSO Lucy finds the enforcement-related powers to be frustrating and limiting:

> You can't detain somebody; you can require that they wait for up to thirty minutes. Who's going to do that? 'Can you just wait here for thirty minutes please whilst a police officer comes along to arrest you?' It's not going happen but we can't physically detain them unless under your common law powers, but that's only if you catch them actually committing an offence. So that's an issue, not being able to search for us is an issue, and fixed penalty notices for a lot of things. We can give them, for a few things, but certainly the vehicle ones, you can only issue for parking offences. And the amount of people we see on mobiles phones and things like that, or with the kids in the car with no seatbelts on, that's something that really annoys me. I think we should be able to deal with them. (PCSO Lucy, Marshton)

Like Lucy, several PCSOs felt that their job would be easier if they could have just a few additional powers so that they would not need police officers to intervene as frequently. These officers align to Cosgrove's (2015) 'Frustrated' PCSO typology in that their role orientation is primarily with the enforcement elements of the job, and thus they find their lack of powers limiting. Other PCSOs felt that any addition to their range of powers or equipment would change the very nature of the role, such as PCSO Ellie:

> If you think about if they're going to give you powers to detain and give you handcuffs, they're going to have to give you batons because that job can escalate in seconds. If you're searching someone, they might not like that, and then things could escalate. So it's where do you start and where do you finish? We are not there for that, we are there to be in the community, to be out and about in the community. Even though you do come across things, like people with cannabis, and you just hope that, there again, it's your communication skills, how you talk to them, how you are with them, to keep them there as long as you can and get the details off them. (PCSO Ellie, Fallhill)

For PCSOs like Ellie, even though some elements of the role are frustrating, it is preferable to keep the job as non-confrontational as possible in order to protect the community engagement elements of their work. It is to a more detailed look at these tasks that we will now turn.

Community engagement

While crime-related and enforcement work is a part of the PCSO role, community engagement tasks are an equal, if not greater, aspect of what PCSOs do. While there will be a degree of overlap between the two, community engagement is an important, if somewhat undervalued, component to the work of the PCSO, and the core activity here is high-visibility patrol (Cosgrove and Ramshaw 2013).

While some aspects of patrol were discussed above in relation to enforcement, there is a great deal more to this task. PCSOs regard patrol as essential to the success of their work generally, as it is through patrolling and speaking to local residents and businesses that PCSOs learn about their beat areas, the people in them, and the events taking place. Police officers, such as PC Joshua, also acknowledge the importance of patrol:

> [PCSOs] can help us out a lot by collecting evidence, speaking and doing house to house enquiries, collecting CCTV and some of the tasks that might tie me up and frees me up a bit more to do other tasks that PCSOs can't do. […] But there's a lot of roles that PCSOs do that I just don't get chance to do. […] The PCSOs can spend more time out in the community doing jobs which some people think, 'oh they're not doing much'. But they are walking round, they're talking to shop

keepers, they're going in schools and they're building up trust with the community and they find a lot of intelligence out. […] If the PCSOs weren't doing it, myself and my colleagues don't get time to do it. […] We rely on them to do the house to house enquiries and revisits to victims of crime, and offer help and support to people. […] They are out there a lot, people do know them, I can go around the community and people don't always know me but they know the PCSOs because they're there all the time, and they know them by first name. (PC Joshua, Starrybridge)

As PC Joshua indicates, it is the ability of PCSOs to build a degree of social capital with the residents and business owners in their beat areas that enables many of their other tasks, such as gathering intelligence (discussed earlier) and addressing neighbour disputes. 'Social capital' refers to social networks which a person has that can be utilized to achieve certain goals (Field 2008). By enhancing their social capital in their beat areas, PCSOs know to whom they should speak for certain kinds of information or to address certain local problems. These networks are built up over a period of time as residents, public sector partners, and business owners come to know the local PCSOs. PCSOs and PCs also reported that a less tangible, but important, outcome of patrol is the building of trust between the community and members of the police. PCSO Matt found this when he lost social capital moving from one police beat area to another:

PCSO Matt is still getting to know this area. In his last area, he 'knew who he needed to know'. He has lost all that now after moving to this station, which was due to an internal restructure in the police. Matt says it takes a while to build up trust in an area and to get to know people well. Once a woman with information about local drug dealing rang up the police station where he had worked previously but would only give the information to Matt, not even to the detective constable who took the call. Matt was the one she knew and trusted. It was good information and led to an arrest. Matt feels trust is really important in the job. (Field note 7/02, Wellspring)

The (official) inability of PCSOs to become involved in confrontation and their lack of power of arrest are often cited as weaknesses of the role (e.g. Caless 2007). However, as PC Peter indicates below, the non-threatening nature of the PCSO means that some members of the public will find them more approachable and trustworthy, which has a wider benefit to policing in general:

But yes, they are the eyes and ears on the street, if you like, they are the ones that have formed some fantastic bonds with people in the community, and can get that information because people, largely, trust them. They're not necessarily there as an enforcement tool, they're there to reassure, build bridges, and help our communities grow and be safer communities. (PC Peter, Hedgebourne)

Research by Cosgrove and Ramshaw (2013) supports this view of PCSOs as ideally placed to facilitate connections between the police and communities which are more difficult to access. However, from the interviews and field observations conducted for the current study, it became clear that the trust which PCSOs can engender through building social capital in their beat areas is often specific to them and does not necessarily generalize to the police as a whole. This is reflected in the story of PCSO Matt (above) and from a conversation with PCSO Jacob:

One PCSO, Jacob, mentioned to PCSO Alfie that a local resident had mistaken Jacob for Alfie. He spoke to her and she said he had information for Alfie, but would not give it to anyone else. Trust is clearly very important. (Field note 7/03, Fayhaven)

As trust is not necessarily easily transferable to other police officers and staff, it reflects the importance of PCSOs having the same beat areas for a long period of time and having opportunities to be visible and active in those areas in order to make the needed connections with residents which will build trust. When PCSOs are abstracted to do tasks in other beat areas (such as hot spots patrolling), this undermines the ability of PCSOs to make and maintain that social capital and the trust which can develop from it.

However, while social capital can be beneficial for some people, it can be used in a punitive way against others (Fulkerson and Thompson 2008). There is a danger that that 'intelligence' which PCSOs gather from the residents who trust them will be used against groups who do not regularly engage with the police, such as young people. This is illustrated in the following interview extract from a PC:

Say if some information comes to light about some kids hanging about, or the example I gave where somebody comes in to report a suspicious incident, I could say to the local PCSO 'somebody has reported that there's loads of kids hanging about on such a street and she thinks they're dealing drugs. What do you know about that'? And see if they've heard anything to add to it or if they already know about it. Often they already know because their ears are closer to ground than ours because they're always there. […] They get all the information just in general conversation with people, day to day. (PC Sarah, Hedgebourne)

While the report of young people dealing drugs may not necessarily be inaccurate, the challenge here for PCSOs will be to ensure they strike a balance of engagement and enforcement with these groups so as not to privilege relationships with those who do not challenge the police. PCSOs are aware of this dilemma, and many take steps to ensure that they do not always approach young people in a punitive way. See for example PCSO Paul from Marshton:

It's also working with the youth as well, I've always been a people person, and I've always liked being out there speaking to people. And it's also, like I said, the kids come from quite deprived backgrounds, some of them, and sometimes it's not just about criminalising the kids, sometimes it's about supporting them as well, those that are causing the problems. So getting them into other activities, like I was talking about, we do [an initiative with the local professional football club], so we try and get referrals to them from some of the kids that are causing problems. And we have the youth bus on a Friday night or different nights of the week where we have got game consoles on there to try and get them off the streets. So I enjoy all that side of stuff with it as well. (PCSO Paul, Marshton)

Building social capital through patrol serves other purposes besides intelligence gathering. When PCSOs were asked what sort of tasks they undertake while on patrol, many mentioned checking on vulnerable residents. This would often mean elderly residents, although not exclusively. Some PCSOs will have care homes for the elderly or the disabled on their beats, which they go into a few times a month to see if there have been any issues. Many also reported having a few homes in their areas where they know the resident is an older person who lives alone. They will check on these residents regularly and are often invited in for a cup of tea. If the resident reports a problem related to crime or safety, PCSOs will look into what assistance they or partner agencies can offer, such as PCSO Ellie did for an elderly woman:

I think the job is very rewarding, can be. I think being out in the community, getting to know your beat, getting to know the members of the public, getting to know your community. Going into residential homes, I have two, I have one over on X Road, and I have one here. So I tend to go to, especially the one on X Road, they've had ten break-ins with the last year and we have got a few residents there with mental health issues as well. So yes, they all like to see you and have a chat with you. […] Just before Christmas I had a lady just down the road, and she's eighty seven, and she was a victim of crime. [Ellie describes a distraction burglary from a cold caller.] I went round to see her, gave her a bit of crime prevention advice, made sure she was ok. I found out she lived on her own, late eighties, still got all her marbles, so she said that she had problems walking up the stairs at night and coming down takes her half an hour. She suffers with arthritis in her legs as well. So I thought what can I do for this woman? So I got her a home link alarm around her neck so she if she falls, that's the council, they do a 24 hour call out thing, so all she does is press the cord. They have cords around the house, upstairs and downstairs, and she has one round her neck, so if she falls she just presses it. (PCSO Ellie, Fallhill)

PCSO Ellie went on to describe how she also arranged for new locks to be put in all the exterior doors to help the elderly resident feel secure, and a stair lift to be installed so that she can remain in her own home longer. Ellie found council funding to pay for these and kept the family informed. While this may be an extreme example of what PCSOs can do in their local communities for vulnerable residents, it shows what can be achieved in the role if staff are given the time and resources to do it (Cosgrove and Ramshaw 2013; O'Neill 2014b).

PCSOs make a point of checking on both local businesses and local residents, especially those which are known to be targeted by shoplifters. In some areas a 'shopwatch' scheme has been set up where the businesses who subscribe to it have a direct line of communication with the police and with each other. If one has been targeted for theft, they will warn the other shops and the NPT. Some PCSOs had also set up 'known offender' lists, which are given to shop managers to help them identify potential shoplifters, such as PCSO Paul did in Marshton:

The local Tesco has big shoplifting problem. PCSO Paul helps to update the known offender profile that is kept at the security desk. We went into the shop and Paul chatted to the security guy on the door, and asked if there were any current issues. Data protection is an issue with this profiling system - the Tesco manager had to sign a form to allow them to have the profile book. It can only be viewed in controlled situations. Security staff will consult it if they catch an offender who is not one they already know. (Field note 22/11, Marshton)

Other PCSOs will call into shops at regular intervals during their shift that have ongoing problems with shoplifters or young people hanging around outside, which can seem threatening or older residents. PCSO Dave (field note 19/10, Fallhill) finds that shop workers will sometime report issues to him that are happening in their own residential neighbourhoods because it is safer to do so at work than to be seen speaking to a PCSO at home.

PCSOs are often tasked with making door-to-door enquiries and to do leaflet drops, called 'cocooning'. When a house or car has been burgled, the PCSOs will knock on the doors of the houses in the surrounding area, about five to each side and ten houses opposite. They will ask if residents had seen or heard anything during the time of the burglary and will give crime prevention advice. PCSOs also visit the crime victim, as PCSO Holly described to me during an observation in Starrybridge:

They also do follow-ups after someone is a victim of crime. The PCSOs make sure the victims are taking steps to be more secure and keep them posted on the case. The idea for the operation today was to look out for vulnerability to burglary. Holly knocked on the door and gave advice to houses that she felt were vulnerable. She was looking for things like open doors or windows, or valuables on display. She also knocked on doors near to where a recent burglary was to inform them of the event and urge greater security steps. (Field note 5/12, Starrybridge)

This type of door-to-door work can lead to good information about an ongoing investigation or help the NPT develop a picture of crime patterns in the local area. However, it is a time-consuming and monotonous task and one which police officers do not have the time to do. This type of work also helps PCSOs to develop their social capital in their beat areas, unless they have been brought into a neighbouring beat to increase the police presence and are thus taken away form their own usual patrol area.

All of the activities above relate to patrol in some way and reflect the centrality of this method to the daily work of a PCSO. There are other tasks which PCSOs perform which are not based on patrol, however. For example, several of the NPTs have Home Watch or E-Watch systems set up with residents in their beat areas. Home Watch relies on one home agreeing to be a point of contact with the NPT. If a crime issue arises in their area, the PCSOs will inform the contact who then shares the information with other local residents. This could include the description of suspected burglars who, if spotted, should be reported to the local police. The E-Watch system is an electronic newsletter which is sent to any resident who has provided the NPT with their e-mail address. It performs a similar role to Home Watch and is an opportunity for the NPT to report back to residents on work they are doing to improve safety in the neighbourhood. One of the rural areas I observed had developed a Farm Watch system, which is similar to Home Watch but will be specific to farm-related crimes. As the farms are more dispersed geographically than are houses in a suburban area, it took a great deal of time and effort on the part of the PCSOs to get the Farm Watch system established. While these 'watch' systems can be time consuming to set up and keep running, the PCSOs seemed to feel they were worth it to keep local communities engaged with the police and aware of current crime issues which may affect them. There were even a couple stories of how suspects were caught because of the Home- or E-Watch bulletins.

In addition to the various 'Watch' systems, PCSOs perform other roles which are not directly related to patrol. These include attending community meetings or events, speaking to schoolchildren, resolving neighbour disputes, and attending to general quality-of-life issues. Community events can include meetings which the PCSOs organize to inform communities of crime prevention advice and current issues in the area, as well as to give residents an opportunity to report issues to them. These are events such as the regular Police and Communities Together meetings. PCSOs also have more ad hoc day 'surgeries' which they set up in local supermarkets to reach people who may not attend planned meetings. In addition, PCSOs make a point of attending and being involved in social events in their beat areas, as PCSO Holly describes:

I like working the community events that we get up here through, I would say, from May up until August, there's more or less something going on in the villages here, it's quite a touristy place so we get a lot of people from outside the area coming into the villages. So those types of events, I think, even though it's working, it's not, if you understand what I mean because we can get involved. It's a way, again, for us to get involved and to show the villagers that we are not just here for the policing issues; we are here to get involved with community events basically. (PCSO Holly, Starrybridge)

Other ways PCSOs reach out to their communities is through involvement in local schools. Some of this was addressed above in relation to crime control and crime prevention. However, PCSOs also make a point of finding ways to regularly engage with schools and in particular, primary schools, to establish positive relationships between children and the police. PCSO Deborah finds this to be one of the best aspects of her job:

It's nice going into your schools and doing a bit of work with the kids and it's really nice when you build up that relationship with the kids in the schools and then they see you on the streets and they come and speak to you. That's really nice. (PCSO Deborah, Marshton)

During the course of this research, PCSOs were invited into primary schools to speak about issues of 'stranger danger', road safety, how to get in touch with the police, and who their local officers are. The children would then be offered the opportunity to go sit in the police car and push some of the buttons, much to their great delight. PCSOs who remain in one area for a long period of time can come to learn who the young people in their area are and will in fact watch them transition to adulthood. This was especially the case in the more rural areas (although as Merritt [2010] has argued, this is becoming increasingly rare as many PCSOs now leave after a few years to become police officers). This local knowledge and social capital can be useful should the young people later become involved in ASB or other problematic activities. For example:

We were discussing the young people in town. PCSO Holly says she knows them as they grow up. If they are involved in crime or ASB, she can identify them a mile off, even by their gait. Response officers wouldn't know them and the line of enquiry would be lost if only they responded. (Field note 7/12, Starrybridge)

This is not to suggest that these relationships are entirely punitive in their motivation. PCSO Holly also talked about how she attended the funeral of a local boy who had committed suicide and the positive impact her presence there had on her relationships with the other young people.

It is not just young people who can have problematic behaviour that requires the intervention of a PCSO. Several of the PCSOs I observed were or had been involved in trying to resolve disputes between neighbours. This can include issues such as one neighbour's CCTV system recording activities beyond their property line, the alleged vandalism of a pavement lighting system, and smoke drifting from regular rubbish burning in an allotment into a neighbour's home. These disputes could take several days if not weeks to resolve and were generally not tasks which the PCSOs enjoyed. However, these were matters which were having an impact on the quality of life of the residents, many of whom were grateful for the PCSOs getting involved. Police officers also saw the value in this type of work, which may seem trivial at surface level:

> We have had incidents in the past where if you get two neighbours together that are both quite unreasonable and illogical then neither can ever see the other persons point of view, so it has got the potential to escalate where they're causing damage to each other's property, you've got offences being committed. But if that can be nipped in the bud at the start by some mediation from a PCSO or going to the next level which is formal mediation, then a lot of issues can be resolved. (PC Sarah, Hedgebourne)

While problems like neighbour disputes and other small quality-of-life issues are not sufficiently serious to require a police officer to attend, they can, as PC Sarah indicates, grow into more serious problems if not addressed. PCSO Nieve recognizes that what is a small matter to her might be a very large problem to someone else:

> It might seem a silly little problem that they've got, like an old lady complaining about kids throwing stones at her window, but to that old lady, it's a big problem and it's bothering her and it's affecting her life so I never rubbish any incidents, I always think something's made them ring up. Some people are intolerant of young people and they do ring up for no reason, but some old people are genuinely frightened of what we see as just a trivial incident. And I think if they didn't have PCSOs, those people wouldn't get seen, nobody would get to see those people. So we do deal with the low level stuff but I think we serve a purpose. (PCSO Neive, Wellspring)

By having the time and the resources, through the work of PCSOs, to respond to these types of calls, the NPT can build positive relationships with local communities, gather information on local problems, and increase trust in the police (Cosgrove and Ramshaw 2013; O'Neill 2014b). However, funding cuts and staff shortages since the time of this research have made this type of policing more difficult to achieve, as will be addressed in Chapter 7.

Administrative tasks

While crime control and community engagement are the main foci for PCSOs, their administrative roles cannot be dismissed. Every PCSO starts and ends the day in the police station, and it is during these periods (and sometimes at points in between) that PCSOs attend to office-based tasks. This will include signing in and out of the police systems, checking e-mail, attending the daily briefing (and in some places leading the daily briefing), preparing neighbourhood newsletters, updating social media, inputting intelligence and other information into the databases, writing statements, and attending team meetings. As was discussed above, PCSOs will also occasionally need to prepare bulk mailings which they may hand deliver during their patrols, or prepare leaflet drops for cocooning tasks. As PCSOs are meant to spend the majority of their time outside, there is usually pressure from managers to do these tasks quickly. However this is not always possible, as PCSO Holly discusses:

> Sometimes now, it can be an hour or two hours before we manage to get out of the door at the beginning of a shift due to updates that we have to do on things like Facebook, Twitter, the E-Watch, the Home watch, newsletters that we have to produce, crime figures that we have to send out to people. And sometimes it can be really time consuming especially because I work on a team where there's only two PCSOs, and only one of us has got access to the Facebook etc. (PCSO Holly, Starrybridge)

These desk-based administrative tasks are also a form of community engagement. However, in PCSO Holly's experience, being more connected to communities through the Internet and social media has the ironic effect of preventing her from achieving as much face-to-face contact with those communities on foot patrols as she would like.

Once PCSOs do make it out of the office, they will also be tasked with certain transportation errands, such as collecting CCTV evidence that police officers need for an investigation or taking evidence to a storage facility. Both of the police forces I observed conducted regular questionnaires of local residents to ascertain their views of policing, and it was usually the task of PCSOs to administer these questionnaires. The staff would be given a list of addresses to target, although they were allowed to attempt the property on either side if there was no answer at the listed address. The questionnaire can be given to the resident to complete directly, or the PCSO will ask the questions and write the answers. Both methods are usually conducted inside the resident's home, rather than on the doorstep. PCSO Ellie describes the survey and finds it to be worthwhile:

> [T]he neighborhood survey comprises of four different sections which is you asking the particular resident of this address what they think of the police, have they got any issues. One of the sections is about their area, any problems with littering, noise nuisance, neighbor disputes, wheelie bins being set on fire and little things like that. A section of the survey is about the criminal justice system, how fair do you think it is, if they have any issues and what they are. I feel they are quite a good tool to use because not everyone will stop you in the street and tell you if they've got something going on next door or next door but one that they want to raise. Not everyone will pick the phone up, where I think if you go into somebody's home environment, they're more relaxed and they're more likely to tell you stuff then being out on the streets where other people may be able to hear you. You do get quite a lot of information out of people, and it's a good thing really because they might never have seen you before because they may have never had to ring the police before, and not everyone looks out of their window twenty four hours a day. So it's about putting a name to your face and introducing yourself. There's a lot of people, when you actually go to do neighborhood surveys and your actually talking to people, and I always like to ask 'do you know how to contact us if you have to?', and some people say 'no, I only know the 999 number'. So that's a good thing to give them information, give them our number here, give them your details, and also give them the 101 number which is the non-emergency number. So they get something out of it as well because they now know who you are. (PCSO Ellie, Fallhill)

While many PCSOs agreed with Ellie about the value of the questionnaires and did not mind doing them, not all PCSOs were quite as enthusiastic about the surveys. Some discussed how residents will get off topic when discussing their views and thus keep the

PCSOs away from their beats and other tasks for an extended period. No PCSO reported having any training on how to do the surveys and some did acknowledge that it must be difficult for some residents to be honest about their feelings about the police with a member of that force asking the questions (field notes 1/10 and 8/10, Fallhill).

Emergency-related work

The final category of PCSO tasks relates to those where PCSOs are involved in assisting with emergencies. Officially, PCSOs are not permitted to be the first on the scene of Grade 1 calls (the most serious emergency situations which require an immediate response). However, several PCSOs mentioned being first on the scene in emergencies either because this was during the early years of PCSOs when their purpose was still somewhat unclear, because the dispatch operator who sent them misunderstood the nature of the call, or because they happened to be close to the incident when the call came in. In the case of the latter, PCSOs will sometimes position themselves near to the event but out of sight, so that they can identify the suspects later or assist in locating suspects if they attempt to flee. There are other occasions where members of the public upon seeing them on patrol have asked them to intervene in a situation, and they did not feel able, on moral grounds, to walk away. PCSO Chris describes an incident where he and two PCSO colleagues were driving in a police van and happened upon a shop where an assault had just taken place:

> I was first on the scene to a stabbing victim who was covered in lots of blood, he had a nasty wound to his tricep which was sort of hanging off, and he'd also been stabbed in the upper abdomen. I didn't know where the knife had gone, all I could see was the puncture wound. So I got an ambulance for him, I got him to hold on to that bit himself, put pressure on that, and I put some pressure on his wound here. But at the time, I thought that this guy could die here because of the amount of blood he was losing. The paramedics were there immediately, more or less took two or three minutes, and it turned out the knife had clipped his liver but from what I could see, my first thoughts were it could've got his heart. So it was a bit awkward, and it's always nice when the paramedics come to take over in situations like that. I had another guy who collapsed, in these medical type of situations you find yourself there before the paramedics. (PCSO Chris, Hedgebourne)

Like police officers, PCSOs also find the 'action' aspects of the job exciting (Reiner 2010; Merritt 2010; Cosgrove 2015) and may at times be keen to get involved in events even when strictly speaking they should not do so. For example, PCSO Joe recalls the following event where he and a colleague responded to an event in progress because they were close by and no police officer was available:

Last week we dropped on and there was a street robbery, somebody had been quite severely beaten, and there was nobody else shouting up for it, and we were just in the area. Normally we wouldn't go to it because it's an immediate, but there was nobody else so I shouted up and I went to that, and then there was a description of the vehicle and we passed one coming the opposite way so we span round, directed officers in, they stopped it. So that sort of stuff, it's a bit more exciting. (PCSO Joe, Hedgebourne)

In cases like this, the PCSOs will stay at the event and try to maintain the situation until police officers arrive. Once police constables have addressed the immediate incident, PCSOs may be called upon to help with the ongoing situation, such as through scene guarding or maintaining road closures. This is a more orthodox use of their role as it does not involve immediate danger. PCSOs who are tasked with guarding a scene take a log of who enters and leaves the scene, although, as some PCSOs noted, they do not actually have the power to stop anyone from entering a crime scene. PCSOs may also be tasked with running an information point after an event, as PCSO Steve describes:

[Y]ou can be stood in the scene, you could be manning a pod, if there's been one set up, like say when there was a murder at the petrol station around the corner, you stick a pod there so you can be on there. A pod is a mobile police station, it's really like a trailer, they pull up, it comes off the back of a wagon, put it down, mobile office, we call them police pods. You could be on there so you're dealing with members of the public coming and asking or if they want to give any information and you're there to reassure them. (PCSO Steve, Marshton)

This type of community engagement and reassurance work is more aligned to the purpose of PCSOs rather than standing at a fixed point for an extended period, taking a note of people coming and going. However, this type of 'filling-in' work is something that PCSOs are often tasked to do to save a police officer from doing it. This applies to road closures and where PCSOs may be used to direct traffic away from an inaccessible road because of weather conditions or because an incident has occurred there. Normally PCSOs do not have the power to stop or redirect moving cars, but the case of road closures is an exception.

A final type of emergency work where PCSOs are used to increase the numbers of officers present is during searches for missing persons. In these cases there will be several police officers from a variety of units involved, as well as PCSOs searching a specific area. PCSO Ellie mentioned enjoying the teamwork involved in these events and hearing the developments unfold on the radio (field note 9/10, Fallhill).

Communication and Local Knowledge

So far this chapter has considered the work that PCSOs do in their daily routine: enforcement-related activity, community engagement work, administrative tasks, and some emergency-response activity. Cutting across all of these are two themes which emerged repeatedly in conversations during fieldwork and in interviews: the importance of communication skills and the importance of local knowledge for PCSOs. Communication was often identified by PCSOs as a core skill for them to master in their role. For example:

MO: What are the tools in your toolbox that you use most?
Communication is a big one definitely, and how you talk to people. Like we were saying the other day, you go in to a group of kids in a park, and if you go in like a bull in a china shop, you're going to get it back aren't you? So you're best off going in down there and working your way up to bring them down to your, to get a happy medium. I think it is all about communication, talking, talking to people and listening to them as well, but also you obviously communicating with them and stuff. (PCSO Ellie, Falllhill)

MO: When you think about the work that you do, what sorts of skills do you think you use the most?

Communication skills, your mouth more than anything, you do talk to a lot of people every day, and I would say that is the most valuable skill. If you can't speak to people doing this job, then you won't be able to do this job. There are obviously other skills that you pick up or you've already got in your locker but I would say your communication skills are, by far, the most important. (PCSO Jeffery, Fayhaven)

Police constables also mentioned communication as a key part of PCSOs' work, both in terms of generally being effective in their jobs but also in relation to gathering useful intelligence to bring back to the police station.

MO: In your opinion, what makes for a really good PCSO, what sorts of skills should be there?
Good communication skills. I think they've got to be very thick skinned because they get a lot of abuse sometimes, probably more so that we do. And so because of that I think they need to be very patient and tolerant. A lot of people they deal with are young people and so particularly in that area, I think that's why the communication needs to be confident and effective. (PC Cathy, Hedgebourne)

They just have to be able to listen to what people are saying and they have to be able to communicate to them and to us really, feel confident that what they've gathered is valuable and share it. And to be the kind of person who you'd be happy to come to speak to you. (PC Ben, Marshton)

Closely linked to communication is the ability of PCSOs to develop and share local knowledge of people and places. As the quote from PC Ben above indicates, this knowledge is seen as valuable for intelligence purposes within the organization, but it also is described as valuable by PCSOs so that they can more effectively serve their beat area in whatever capacity they are needed. By having a good working knowledge of who the local residents are, how the area is laid out, what the problematic places are, and how these all converge, they feel they are best placed to address local issues such as neighbour disputes, ASB, and working with young people. For example, PC Joshua initially joined his police force as a PCSO and felt that knowledge of people and places is core to the work of a PCSO:

Just knowing the area, knowing people in the area. I think once you know the area and people know you, then the community trust you and they tell you stuff and you find information out. It can be the most basic thing of who's living in a certain house, it's like PCSO Charlie now, he's collecting a CCTV rota and it's quite a basic thing but he's come up with the idea of making this spreadsheet of where all the CCTV is in the area. And he knows now as soon as a break-in has happened on there, we got to Charlie and say 'Charlie, where are the cameras?', and he knows, its knowing your area I think. (PC Joshua, Starrybridge)

PCSO Henry likewise feels building knowledge of local people is the fundamental task of a PCSO. Being familiar to local residents encourages trust, and from trust comes the willingness to share information.

MO: How important is it for your job to get to know people in the area and how things work around here?
It's vital. If you can't integrate yourself into an area effectively, and open lines of information sharing and two way communication, then you've no business being a PCSO because that's how we gather intelligence as to what's going off within the community, who's doing what. Because people will talk to us as opposed to a police officer [...] and they get to know your face, and that comes from you talking to people, introducing yourself, and as that builds as time goes on, you gain peoples trust, and once you've done that, you've integrated yourself within the community, people know you, your name, your face, and they know if you're telling you something in confidence, then that confidence is not betrayed. But whatever they do tell us, we can disseminate what's relevant and what isn't, and feed that into the organisation on our intelligence system. (PCSO Henry, Wellspring)

For PCSO Matt, having local knowledge also assists PCSOs in dealing with the limitations of their powers:

So you might have stopped them for one offence, and you know it's a man called Jonny Smith from 11 Main Avenue, he's not going to stop, 'no I'm going, sorry mate but I'm going', and he's gone. But the thing is I know who he is because I've dealt with him before, going back to knowledge, I've dealt with him before and we will go along later on and sort it out. (PCSO Matt, Wellspring)

As the above indicates, the aspects of the PCSO role highlighted by both PCSOs and police officers as vital to its success are communication and local knowledge of people and places. Being good communicators involves both listening skills and interaction with community members, as well as achieving good communication within the police origination itself. These skills then enable increased trust (internally and externally) and an increase in local knowledge, both in terms of knowing people and places and being given potentially useful information on crimes in the area which they can effectively share with relevant police colleagues. This puts PCSOs in the position of being *professional knowledge brokers*. In the past police officers have been referred to as knowledge brokers, especially in the context of partnership work (Ericson 1995; Crawford 1997; Hughes and Rowe 2007) where they will negotiate information and information sharing between a variety of public and private-sector agencies. For PCSOs, the brokering of knowledge is between members of the public in their beat areas and with other police officers and staff within the organization. While police officers may be more interested in information that relates to criminal activity (see also Cosgrove and Ramshaw 2013), PCSOs value the local knowledge which does not meet this criteria but nonetheless increases their own understanding of what is happening locally and who is involved.

This is of course the ideal situation. Not all PCSOs will master this level of local integration nor develop sufficient trust within the police organization to share the information they do have effectively. The conclusion will reflect on this in terms of its significance for the remainder of the book.

Conclusion

PCSOs were introduced to policing in England and Wales with a view to providing police officers with some additional support in their work in communities. They are intended to operate at a slower pace than police officers do and to conduct high-visibility foot patrol for the majority of their shift time. The role has developed over the years, and this chapter has considered the kinds of tasks and routines in which PCSOs were engaged during the course of my research with them. Much of their work can be classed as enforcement related, community engagement, administrative, or emergency related. The amount of time that they spend on each of these types of tasks will vary depending on local conditions, personal preferences, and level of demand. Throughout all of these tasks, PCSOs are expected to be building knowledge and connections in their beat areas so that they have a detailed understanding of the people and places that they encounter most often. In order to do this, both PCSOs and police officers identified good communication and listening skills as vital aspects of the role. These are utilized both with community members and within the police organization itself in order to effectively share any knowledge of criminal activity which has been gained. In this regard, it is argued that PCSOs operate as professional knowledge brokers between communities and the police.

However, it must be acknowledged that this chapter is a detailed examination of the ideal situation, the 'Professional' PCSO in Cosgrove's typology (2015). Not all PCSOs will be able to achieve a high level of integration within communities or within their police forces. This will be due to a variety of factors, such as inadequate social capital development, poor communication skills, a lack of interest in the role [all of these reflecting Cosgrove's 'Disillusioned' PCSO (2015)], or an orientation towards applying for a police officer position and thus departure from the role after a short period [Cosgrove's 'Frustrated' PCSO (2015)]. Regardless of whether the ideal-type PCSO was achieved, this is the image which PCSOs wish to present to others, and it is the standard against which they are held. As one PC said to me, it only takes one PCSO to be seen to fail in this regard for all of them to be tarred with the same brush (PC Stuart, Marshton).

What has been presented in this chapter is the ideal *definition of the situation* for PCSOs (Goffman 1959). As was explored in Chapter 2, this refers, in dramaturgical terms, to the performance that PCSOs wish to give to those not within their performance team. It shows them to be competent members of the policing organization, skilled in communication techniques, and with a depth of local knowledge that is unachievable for police officers. This is the *presentation of self* which PCSOs seek to display every day that they are at work, and as the next two chapters will explore, it is the self they have to defend every day from challenge from both police officers and the organization as a whole. Chapter 4 will consider how from the point of application and through to their first forays on the beat PCSOs are undermined at a structural level by the very organization which has hired them. Chapter 5 will examine the personal interactions between PCSOs and police officers to reveal the composition of the performance teams in community policing and the extent to which they are hostile to each other.

4

Becoming a Police Community Support Officer and Being Institutionally Undermined

This chapter will consider the process of becoming a Police Community Support Officer (PCSO), from deciding to apply for the position (which in many cases involved leaving another field of work), to the initial training experiences, and the first few months of shadowing experienced colleagues on foot patrol in neighbourhoods. The focus of this chapter is on the initial relationship between the individual PCSOs and the institution which they have now joined: i.e. the organizational socialization process (Chao et al 1994). The chapter considers the stages of initiation into community policing which PCSOs experienced and the moments along the way where the organization failed to fully equip these new recruits with the tools they would need to give convincing *performances* (in the dramaturgical sense, as was described in the Chapter 3) as accepted members of the police team. While work as a PCSO was attractive to these individuals for a variety of reasons which will be explored, the reality upon entering the occupation was that many were, to an extent, left to learn for themselves how to do the work, as the organization itself had not given consistent messages in this regard or adequate support in order for them to learn in a formal capacity how to do the job.

This chapter starts to explore how the police organization has *institutionally undermined* the role of PCSO from the beginning, a situation which, during the time of the research, was continuing to a degree in relation to a lack of resource available for ongoing training and development. Examples to illustrate these processes are drawn from observations and interviews with the PCSOs and police officers from the six neighbourhoods which were studied for this research, as described previously. Throughout the chapter, reference is made, where appropriate, to how Goffman's dramaturgy illustrates the impact of this institutional undermining on the PCSOs. However, as this chapter focuses on the effects of institutional-level behaviour, the role of dramaturgy in the analysis will be less prevalent here. The socialization processes which PCSOs encounter in their daily work with police officers and other PCSO colleagues are developed in Chapter 5, where a dramaturgical analysis forms a core component. For now, we begin with a consideration of what motivated the participants in this research to apply for the PCSO position. This will be followed by an examination of their experiences in formal training and the processes by which they entered their first beat assignments.

Deciding to Apply

The PCSOs who participated in this research came from a variety of backgrounds and previous employment experiences. Some had served many years in other areas of work (decades, in a few cases), while others were interested in joining the police as a regular officer, but as they had held few previous jobs, they were advised to serve as a PCSO for a few years to gain more employment experience. Thus the motivation for becoming a PCSO could vary considerably. This section will explore the motivations which the research participants expressed for deciding to apply to be a PCSO, which ranged from 'push' factors (such as being dissatisfied with previous employment), to both instrumental and ideological 'pull' factors (elements of the PCSO job itself which seemed appealing) (see Clary and Synder 1999 and Bullock and Leeney 2014 for studies of similar motivations for volunteers and Special Constables).

Several of the PCSOs who were interviewed identified problems in their previous employment which led them to seek other work. For some, their previous job was about to end because of redundancy or internal reorganization processes, and so they had no option but to seek other employment. Even for those who were not being forced out of a job, there were elements of their work which they found dissatisfying. For example, PCSO Dave left work as a bus driver to be a PCSO:

Because on the bus, driving, you don't really talk to anyone, you are always in your cabin, if someone comes to speak to you, if you have to ask something, you just say, 'Would you like a ticket?', something like that if they need a ticket. Or, 'Can I help you', that's it. And sometimes you get a bad response; someone doesn't pay for the ticket or anything, many frustrating things. (PCSO Dave, Fallhill)

Another PCSO, Matt, had a rewarding career as a self-employed baker but changes in the business forced him to work for supermarkets instead:

Matt was a baker before this job. He had his own shop for a bit, then worked for a couple supermarkets. He found it tedious when working at the distribution factory so he looked for something else. He saw this job advertised and applied. He was put on a waiting list for a few months before he was hired. (Field notes 4/02, Wellspring)

Most of the PCSOs who discussed previous employment had held blue-collar jobs and viewed work as a PCSO as an improvement upon their current employment conditions or as a route to self-development. Participants described these and several other instrumental 'pull' factors during the interviews and observations. For example, a few PCSOs had held other support staff roles within the police organization, such as in dispatch or custody services. For these participants, work as a PCSO was appealing as it did not involve leaving their current employer, but would be the type of work that would utilize some of the skills and knowledge they had developed in their previous roles, as well as providing a new challenge and some personal development. For example:

I'd worked in the control room [dispatch] initially, and I'd done that for about eight years, and after speaking to some other PCSOs I thought it was a good progression to make because I'd spent a lot of time speaking with the public over the phone and speaking with the officers on the radio, that I felt ready and wanted to get out there and make a bit of a difference really. (PCSO Brook, Fayhaven)

Related public sector organizations, such as the local council, also provided future PCSOs:

Before this job I used to work for the local housing for the council, as a warden, and then after that I worked in a social care unit so I was always actually out and about working with people in the community, and I just found it a progression from that really. (PCSO Holly, Starrybridge)

Employment as a PCSO was seen to bring other desirable elements for some staff, such as good pay, a good pension, and improved conditions of service compared to their current roles.

Several participants, such as PCSO Deborah, found the varied nature of the work appealing in that they would be outdoors a good proportion of the time working with a broad cross-section of the public on a variety of issues:

> I used to work in a drug and alcohol service, I enjoyed helping people but I felt a bit more restricted because you're sat behind a desk all the time, and most of these people were involved in crime, and I felt it was a bit limited in what I could do then. So applying for a PCSO, I felt there was more scope to do more work; obviously I could go to people's houses, do more referrals and work with people more on a one to one basis. Obviously enforcing law but also helping them in the social side to try and make them not reoffend or anything like that. (PCSO Deborah, Marshton)

PCSO Gary was also attracted to the active nature of the role:

> So, just out and working with members of the community, people in the community, and being out and about is more my scene anyway than being cooped up in an office or anything like that. (PCSO Gary, Fallhill)

There was one instrumental pull factor which was mentioned more than any other: work as a PCSO was viewed as preparation for future employment as a police constable (see also Cosgrove and Ramshaw 2013). However, this link was made in a variety of ways. Some PCSO applicants had already decided that they wished to join the police as a full police constable, but needed more experience before they would be considered. This assessment could either be one they made themselves or it could come from a police recruitment officer. For example:

> When I was at school my intention was to become a police officer eventually and I started off on the front desk as an enquiry desk assistant and then progressed to a PCSO and then obviously, in hope, in time, that I might become a police officer. (PCSO Grace, Hedgebourne)

PCSO Henry, who is about 10 years older than PCSO Grace, had a different story, in that his initial application to the police failed because of lack of work experience. The development of the PCSO role provided him a way back into the police service:

> I've always wanted to be a police officer, it's one of my ambitions, and it's always been an ambition of mine. I did apply years ago when I was about eighteen/nineteen, and at that time the feedback was I'd not got enough life experience at that point. So having then done a variety of jobs, and gained experience, a PCSO role came up and then I applied and then I've

just taken it from there and just gone another step up the ladder now and applied to become a PC. (PCSO Henry, Wellspring)

For others who joined as a PCSO as a way into the police service, the decision to apply to be a full police constable was not yet firm for them at the time of application. These individuals saw the role as a way to sample policing life without having to make the full commitment as a constable, to aid their decision-making. This is the 'try before you buy' motivation:

PCSO Marie is becoming a PC soon. She says being a PCSO was a great grounding in the job. Others who 'jump right in' to be PCs sometimes find out that it is not for them. PCSOs do the things that PCs don't have the time to do. They get too busy to be out on patrol and speaking to people. (Field notes 27/09, Fallhill)

As this and the following quote suggest, the decision to be a police officer reflects a degree of commitment that becoming a PCSO does not.

MO: But you feel it (being a PCSO) would give someone a good grounding to be a police officer?
Yes I think you'd either think 'oh yes or no', because I started (as a PCSO) with two girls and they wanted to be police officers, and they stayed for two years and they went back to their old jobs because it's not what they thought it was. One went back to be a paramedic and one went back to insurance or something. So I think it all depends on what you're like as a person, as well, if you enjoy the job. (PCSO Ellie, Fallhill)

However, not everyone agreed that employment as a PCSO can give a person an accurate insight into a police officer's working life. The PC below, Beth, felt that not only is it a very different type of work, but working as a PCSO would be frustrating for those who were keen and well-placed to be regular police officers.

(PCSOs) haven't got the powers to deal with offences, so you wouldn't get an insight. You'd get an insight into a police station and how it worked and the community contact points and everything else. But you wouldn't be dealing with stuff like you would a police officer. You wouldn't be working night shifts, you wouldn't be dealing with aggressive people, and you wouldn't be putting yourself in danger. And you've not got the power to deal with somebody. Do you know what I mean? If I had to go through as a PCSO I probably wouldn't stick it for a year because I would hate being on the street and someone talking to me like a piece of shit and not being able to do anything. So I probably wouldn't go for that at all, I wouldn't come through it. (PC Beth, Fallhill)

A third instrumental reason which was identified for joining the police service as a PCSO prior to applying to be a regular police officer was simpler than the two mentioned above: the service had a recruitment freeze on PC roles and work as a PCSO was the only option. During the time of the research, police forces in England and Wales were preparing themselves for the expected 20% funding cut which had been announced by the Conservative-Liberal coalition government in 2010. This meant that many forces were cutting back on new recruits or only recruiting from existing staff (such as PCSOs and Special Constables). This was the case for PCSO Alfie:

MO: Why did you first apply to become a PCSO?
I first applied because they weren't recruiting for PCs at the time and this was the next best option in terms of getting some boxes ticked that may help in order to become a PC at some point in the future. (PCSO Alfie, Fayhaven)

A final instrumental pull factor for joining the service as a PCSO identified by a few respondents was age. Unlike some of the younger recruits who have a clear vision of using the PCSO experience to progress to being a regular officer, such as PCSO Alfie above, other PCSOs joined because they felt they were too old to be a police officer but still wanted to work for the organization. For example, PCSO Neive prioritized having a family before joining the service:

MO: So were you interested in becoming a police officer at one point?
I was at one point but because of my family I kept putting it off and then I decided I was the wrong age to apply, so when this job came up I thought it was great because it's sort of policing but more involved with the community which I like doing that side of it best to be honest. Because I think that's what our job is all about, it's about helping people, it's about reassuring people, it's not all the sexy stuff about chasing cars and giving tickets out, that's a police officer's job, in my view, but I do enjoy the community side of it. I think that's why I applied, because I was labelling myself too old to join the police, I thought this was the next best thing but without actually being a police officer. (PCSO Neive, Wellspring)

For Nieve, being a PCSO gave her a second opportunity to be involved in community policing which she might not have otherwise had. PCSO Chris, below, who also joined the role later in life after many years in factory work, does not feel work as a constable would be appropriate now.

People sometimes say to me 'why don't you apply to be a Bobby', but obviously with my age, what's the point? But I do see it (the PCSO) as a different role. Locking people up and just speaking to people are two different things. (PCSO Chris, Hedgebourne)

For these PCSOs above, the role provided them with clear benefits, in terms of gaining some life experience to use in an application to be a regular police constable, build on existing skills with a new challenge, get better pay, get out from behind a desk, or have a chance later in life to do community policing work. These are all clear instrumental pull factors. However, respondents also identified some of the more idealistic pull factors that drew them into the job. For PCSO Chris, the work of a PCSO was attractive not only because it got him outside, but also because it spoke to his religious values:

The other thing was I felt it would be very worthwhile doing a job where I was helping other people, being a Christian and having Christian values, I believe that being a Christian is about helping other people. And since I've been doing the job I've found that I do get quite a lot of satisfaction knowing that I may have helped people improve their quality of life. (PCSO Chris, Hedgebourne)

PCSO Neive feels that regular police officers are too busy to deal with 'quality-of-life' calls, which, while not relating to a crime as such, can have a large impact on a person's daily life. She feels that PCSOs are a vital resource to communities in that they do have the time for this type of work, which she enjoys.

It frustrates me when people say 'well you can't do anything'. But I say to them what do you mean we can't do anything, and they see it as 'well you can't arrest people' but that's not what our job is about, I don't want to go out arresting people and rolling about on the floor fighting on a Friday night, I want to solve peoples issues that are low level, and that's why we were brought in. […] They're going to just keep giving us a little bit more [powers] and a little bit more, and we are going to end up as a second tier police force. Which will be a shame, a lot of communities will miss out if PCSOs change so much that they're not doing what they were set up to do. (PCSO Neive, Wellspring)

The drive to help members of the community is strong for PCSO Lucy as well. Similar to PCSOs Deborah and Holly, quoted above,

Lucy was in a previous role that involved aspects of health and social care, but she felt work as a PCSO would give her scope to support more people.

MO: Why did you apply to be a PCSO in the first place?
Because I like working with the community, I was working as a nurse at the time. I always fancied the police role but I always wanted to do the community side of the role, being out on the beat, speaking to people that had been victims of crime. So when the PCSO role came out, I thought: you're not tied up with prisoners and dealing with crime all the time, you can be out and about and be on the streets. So that's what appealed to me, that's why I applied for it. (PCSO Lucy, Marshton)

As this discussion has shown, there is a wide range of factors that motivated applications to the PCSO role. Some were 'push' factors in that previous employment was unsatisfactory in some way or had been lost through redundancy. Other applicants were more motivated by 'pull' factors. These could be both instrumental (gaining more challenging employment experience, improved working conditions, or improved chances of future employment as a police constable) and ideological (wanting to help people in the community), and these motivations have also been found among police recruits (see Chan 2003; Fielding 1988; and Cosgrove and Ramsahaw 2013, who find similar patterns for PCSOs). As the PCSO role was only created in 2002, no respondents will have grown up with a 'calling' to become one. Thus most did not see it in those terms, as can be the case for police officers (Crank 2004; Brogden et al 1988). For many, it is a *job*, like any other, and one which they might only do for a short period before moving on to something else. (This is discussed further in Chapter 6.) However, it is interesting to observe the extent to which some respondents viewed their work in the police as an important and valuable community role which they were keen to pursue and which motivated them to apply for the job in the first place. Not all of these respondents retained this commitment to the organization, however (as van Maanen 1975 and Chan 2003 observed with police recruits), and it is to a detailed look of initial PCSO training that we now turn.

Initial Training

After a successful application and interview, newly recruited PCSOs attend a period of classroom training to learn about their role, the practicalities of the job, and what is expected of them from the organization. Participants in this project were asked how long this training lasted and what it included. The responses reveal a wide range of experiences in relation to the formal training component of their initiation into the police. For example, some PCSOs report a formal classroom training period of up to 8 weeks, while others had as little as 3 weeks of training. While there is some inverse correlation in the responses between the duration of training and the PCSO's length of service (in that those who joined in the early years of the role tended to have shorter training periods), this was not always the case. PCSO Charlie, for example, had been in service for 8 years and reported 8 weeks of classroom training, while PCSO Joe, who had joined 5 months previously, had 5 weeks of training. This variation in the length of the classroom training occurred within each police force which was studied, as well as between the police forces.

The content of the training, however, was remarkably similar across the PCSO respondents. For example, PCSO Deborah describes the formal training as:

> It was one day at [the training school for the police officers], that was just an informal day of meeting and greeting and a bit of legislation, and codes of practice. And then when we went onto division, it was a group of about twenty PCSOs [being trained], then we had two teachers, one was based in CID [a detectives] and one was more out and about [...] So we covered quite a lot of topics, it was first aid where they'd people in to come and teach things like that, respect race and diversity, law training, which I had a bit of basic law training. We had a couple of days on each subject, which it probably could've been a bit longer to be honest because it's a lot to take in in a very short amount of time. Self-defence training; we had with officer safety trainers. We did radio waves training, that was quite fun because it's quite daunting using a piece of equipment, and you think 'oh I have no idea how to use this', but it was just nice exercises of trying to find things [...] and being able to be confident to use your radio. So it was a nice safe environment, so if you did mess up, you didn't feel stupid because everyone was in the same boat. [IT training on the force's computer systems], that was two days. (PCSO Deborah, Marshton)

Other PCSOs described similar content in the formal training in relation to safety and self-defence, first aid, race and diversity, using radios and IT equipment, and basic law and PCSO powers. Some of the PCSOs also mentioned role-play elements to the formal training, which were used to learn how to interact with, for example, people with mental health conditions or the elderly, or how to deal with other challenging situations. This could include instruction on how to de-escalate an encounter with an angry or upset member of the public, but not all PCSOs mentioned this component in their list of training topics. In fact, a newer recruit to the PCSO role, Trudy, observed that while her longer-in-service colleague had several role-play components in his training, hers contained very little (suggesting that this training method was being reduced). In addition to the standard training, a few PCSOs had taken up the opportunity to have an intensive course on public speaking to assist them when presenting to community meetings or speaking in schools.

While many PCSOs felt that the formal training was useful to a degree, they found it to be either not long enough, not detailed enough, or not realistic. In relation to the length of the training, PCSO Henry described it this way:

> Initial training was four weeks, which was rushed, condensed, it was very much of a whirlwind romance, if you will. You came out of initial training with your head spinning, and you felt, I would say, not confused but somewhat ill-equipped to deal with some of the situations that you were facing, or some of the situations that you were put in and expected to deal with. (PCSO Henry, Wellspring)

His colleague, PCSO Neive, also felt that the length of training she received was not long enough:

> I was a bit disappointed because we only had four weeks' training, and I was ok because I have a lot of knowledge about the police service and I knew how to use a radio [she had worked in dispatch]. But for somebody coming into the police service from an outside job, I don't think four weeks is a long time. (PCSO Neive, Wellspring)

These and other PCSOs describe entry into the police service as being something of a 'shock' (as did Chan 2003 for police recruits) and that they, or others in their cohort, needed more time to take in and practice all the knowledge and new skills which they are expected to adopt and in which they need to become competent. While some other PCSOs did not have an issue with the length of the training, they did feel that there were elements which were missing. For example, PCSO Ellie was faced with a surprising disconnect between the training and her initial experiences on patrol in the division:

[I had a] six week course which covered really about fixed penalties […] tax discs never got covered […] and then when I got out on the streets it was like 'ooh fill one of these in', and I was like 'ooh what's this, we never covered it in training'. And it was quite a big thing, maybe because my mentor was into pulling cars and going round looking at all the tax discs displayed. (PCSO Ellie, Fallhill)

Another PCSO, Holly, felt that it would have been helpful to have a better awareness of the various social services available in the area before starting on a division, as her role has involved a great deal of partnership work:

I think we should've had more training on the community aspect of things, on how to approach different agencies because a lot of the things that we do are partnership based where we work a lot with local partners. And when you're first thrown into it, you don't know who to approach especially if you haven't got a background in social care or housing or whatever. You don't really know who to approach if you've got a vulnerable, how do you know which of social services to get involved with and you're having to find out a lot of things yourself. (PCSO Holly, Starrybridge)

One of the police constables who was interviewed, PC Joshua, had been a PCSO prior to becoming a police officer. His perspective is thus slightly different, but he identified a gap in training that, if met, would facilitate better collaboration between PCs and PCSOs:

I think, being a PCSO before and being a police officer now, there's areas of training that I needed I think. It's just investigation, the procedures that we go through, without having to do it yourself, without having to go through the crime investigation procedure, you don't realize why certain things are done in a certain way. It's just the way it's worked and the way, it might be an exhibit, why we take a statement in a certain way and how we book it in. […] I think because you don't do it as a PCSO, you don't realize how to do certain investigations. Because you've never been trained in it, you don't know what to do, there should be a bit more training there so then you [police officers] can utilize them a bit more, or they can help you out a little bit more than they probably could do. (PC Joshua, Starrybridge)

During the course of my observations, there were indeed occasions where PCSOs were asked to rewrite statements they had made because they were missing key information that the police officers needed, reflecting a gap in their knowledge for an important element of their work. This was time that officers had to spend coaching PCSOs, which some seemed to resent. This lack of training on aspects of the role which became prominent features of the PCSOs' work reflects a feeling among some of the staff that their classroom training was, to an extent, not realistic. Most were trained not by PCSOs but by police officers who had not done the work of PCSO themselves and so may not have had a full understanding of the realities of the role. The following extract from field notes reflects this for a new PCSO recruit:

During the dinner break I met a new PCSO, Jacob. He likes the PCSO job. It is quite busy and much better than his previous desk job. He said his training was not really related to the real job, though. They had 6 weeks in a classroom learning what they can and can't do, which is actually really complicated for PCSOs. It is harder to train PCSOs than PCs as the law is clearer in terms of the powers for PCs. He is still confused about what his are. He then had 6 weeks with a tutor which was like starting all over again. Jacob said they didn't have a lot of role play or scenarios in training, so it wasn't very realistic. It made it seem like they should be doing tickets all the time. He feels that if he did that though, they never would get any information from anyone. Jacob says you have to have a balance and decide when it might be better not to use enforcement. (Field notes 4/03, Fayhaven)

For some of the PCSOs who were longest in service, their trainers at times seemed ill-prepared for the task and did not even have a clear sense of what the PCSO role was. PCSO Tom joined 8 years previously and had this experience in his initial training:

We had people turning up to our lessons saying 'you'll have to excuse me, I didn't realise I was doing this lesson today, I don't know anything about PCSOs, I've just been asked at the last minute'. Everything seemed to be a last minute thing. So you got a feeling people were doing it because they'd been asked rather than doing it, it wasn't very well structured at all at the time. (PCSO Tom, Starrybridge)

The lack of awareness in trainers of the reality of the PCSO role was evident for other PCSOs as well. PCSO Lucy joined her force 6 years previously and found that the training did not adequately prepare her for the role. She gives the example of how PCSOs were trained to handle confrontational situations:

[Y]ou were given circumstances, if this happens and that happens what do you do? Call the cops. Ok so we have got to call a cop, and there's not always a cop available, or it can be twenty minutes till that cops available. It's not as simple and as basic as it was made to sound. […] And you can try and resolve it, sometimes that doesn't work, you have to get an officer to come and you might have to wait for them to come down. Whereas in training you were just told 'yeah you call a cop, a cop will come and sort it', and in reality there's not enough police officers to do that. It was all made to sound very nicey. […] I don't think they had an idea of what it was like; I don't think they had a clue. […] At [the training centre] it was just hammered out to us, off you go, and I don't think there was a reality in it. There's too many grey areas, like non confrontation, that's never going to happen. If you're going up to a group of kids, it immediately could be confrontation. It was just made to sound too nice, I don't think it was intentional, I just don't think they had a clue. (PCSO Lucy, Marshton)

In addition to some PCSOs not having training on aspects of their work which became important, some PCSOs had the opposite experience of being trained in tasks which it turned out they were not permitted to do. This situation arose because unlike police officers who have the same range of powers across the country, chief constables have a degree of flexibility in terms of which powers their PCSOs will be granted within their force area (according to the Police Reform Act 2002).[1] In Northport Police force, this resulted in some confusion as to what PCSOs should be trained to do, as PCSO Holly described:

(W)hen we first started [our training] we did crime reports, we took statements, we did statement training, we did crime report training, but we were never able to use it until the last couple of years, so needed refreshing again. At one point we couldn't write our own statements, we had to get an officer to do it, but now, I think it's only our own statements that we can actually do at the minute. […] We can write our own statements but that's only just come in in the last couple of years even though we had the training nine years ago for it. On our initial training course, we have never been able to do it. And we have only just recently, in the last I would say three or four years, been able to take reports for negative line crimes [where there is no known offender or no evidence].

The PCSOs discussed above have described an organization which, in their view, did not adequately prepare them for their new role. This could be reflected in short formal training periods which did

[1] This situation has become even more complex with the introduction of The Policing and Crime Act (2017), to be discussed further in Chapter 7.

not allow for adequate development of the new information and skills they needed, training which was missing important elements of their role (or, in some cases, trained them in powers they were not allowed to use), or training which did not adequately reflect the reality of the PCSO task. Some trainers were even openly unprepared for the training sessions, and very few PCSOs reported being trained by other PCSOs.

This suggests that from their very first experiences of being a PCSO, these new staff members were being undermined by the police organization itself. In Goffman's (1959) terms, they were not able to learn their PCSO *performances* to a sufficient degree—even as new recruits—to give a convincing *definition of the situation* for when they were assigned their beat areas (as discussed in Chapter 3). There were too many gaps in their knowledge to know how to perform to the expected standard in the field. Although many may not have realized it at the time, the organization was in effect communicating a message (intentionally or otherwise) that PCSOs are not a priority in terms of devoting the necessary resources and time to allow them to play their role in policing (to develop their performance) to the full extent. While PCSOs may be *of* the police organization, they do not *belong* to it, and are therefore not afforded the full range of knowledge and skills they need to appear competent in their work. PCSOs are clearly not a part of the police *team* in the dramaturgical sense. Manning (1970) has argued, in relation to organizational socialization, that '(s)trangers or new members of an organisation are both a part and not a part of the organisation. They act within the limits of the system but do not share the common-sense knowledge current among other members' (1970: 251). Considering the data collected here, it appears that the police organization is failing to impart the basic elements of the system itself to the new PCSO recruits, and this will inhibit their ability later to develop common-sense knowledge of it.

While the period of classroom training is an important element of a PCSO's introduction to their role and to the police organization more generally, it is not the only phase of training which they receive. Next to be explored in this chapter is the less formal elements of training for PCSOs. This includes a period of shadowing a more experienced colleague, as well as a degree of 'refresher' training. As will be demonstrated, however, this periodic training is not as comprehensive as what is offered to police officers, even within the constraints of the PCSO role. A final component of PCSO learning is that which is done informally 'on the job', and which can inform some of the core elements of the role.

Entering the Field

Towards the end of the formal classroom training period, many PCSOs learned to which neighbourhood area they would be assigned to start their active work in community policing. Some PCSOs were first placed in one area on a temporary basis to observe the work of a police constable and then were transferred to their own permanent division. During the first few weeks of this posting, PCSOs accompanied a serving PCSO or police officer for a period of time to allow them to become more familiar with how foot patrol works in practice, to observe how an experienced officer undertook the daily tasks, and to receive immediate guidance and feedback on how they were performing the PCSO role, how they handled any challenging situations, and the choices they made on a day-to-day basis in the context of their work. Research participants were asked how long this shadowing period lasted, and as with the formal training described above, the length of time varied considerably. Some PCSOs only had 1 to 2 weeks of shadowing, whereas others had 10 to 12 weeks. Current practice in one police force was for the length of the shadowing period to depend on how confident the PCSO was in terms of her or his new role, and so it could be shortened if the PCSO requested it.

The other element of this shadowing training method which was variable was whether new PCSOs shadowed a police officer or another PCSO. For those PCSOs who were longer in service, many reported that they shadowed a police officer because there were no other experienced PCSOs yet in the division for them to observe. For example, PCSO Paul recalls that:

> [O]nce we had finished the classroom based [training] we were allocated our divisions we were going to, so when we arrived at divisions we had a PCSO […] supervisor, and that was a police officer. Because of the time when I joined […] it was when they first had the major influx of PCSOs so on my intake we had about approximately ten of us at my station, and we only had two PCSO supervisors that were police officers. And it was there for them to take us out and about on patrol to basically work with them. That lasted for a few shifts, it wasn't like a set period, but then we were left to it really. (PCSO Paul, Marshton)

For other PCSOs, a period of shadowing a police officer was a deliberate choice by the organization because there were officers who were specifically trained to be PCSO tutors. For PCSO Deborah, this was a preferable system:

So when we come onto division from our training, which I was, I think my training was for six weeks in the classroom, and then we came onto division and I had two weeks with a police officer in company. I was with her walking round every day and she was encouraging me to use my radio and taking me to jobs and how you result them, and do stop and accounts, and it was all very nerve-wracking but she was really good because she did support us. And she was trained specifically in mentoring PCSOs when they are new onto the division, so she got paid extra to do that, and she did that for a couple of years. […] So you did feel safe [being with a police officer] and then we all got sent onto our team. (PCSO Deborah, Marshton)

Other PCSOs, and especially those who were newer recruits, shadowed experienced PCSOs when they were assigned their divisions. For PCSO Joe, this was the most effective part of the training process:

MO: Do you feel that your formal training helped prepare you for life as a PCSO?
Not really, I think mainly it was actually getting out with the tutor and listening to PCSO Chris, what he said, making notes of the points that he covered when he does speak to people, and then you develop your own way of speaking to people. You won't say exactly the same things, but you cover the main points, I think that was the best part of the training for the actual practical stuff that we do. The other stuff was just background information, what we can do from the classroom training, but once we got out that was the best bit. (PCSO Joe, Hedgebourne)

PCSO Joe was not the only one to mention that the real learning happened out in the field on patrol with their tutor (van Maanen 1975; Paoline 2003), rather than in the classroom. For PCSO Gary, it is the kind of job that can really only be learned in the doing of it:

I suppose it gave me a bit of confidence, the training, in how to deal with certain scenarios. But a lot of it is to do with, until you're actually out there and dealing with it, there's always that little bit there in your mind that nothings ever going to go wrong. So my personal experience is until you're out there and actually doing the job, and dealing with these things in a live situation if you like, that's the best training. (PCSO Gary, Fallhill)

For PCSO Paul, however, while the shadowing process is indeed an important aspect of training, it could be better organized and would be more effective if it was always another PCSO who serves as tutor. However, while police officers are paid extra for taking on the work of a tutor, PCSOs are not:

> [T]here's things on the job that I've just learnt going along. Like different radio techniques, you just pick it up as you go along. I think they should do a lot longer, and you should be out a lot longer in company with, either, a police officer or an experienced PCSO. Like I said, when I first started, I was one of the first so I didn't really have that opportunity to speak to any other PCSOs that had been in the job for long, and to learn from them. So whereas police officers have a tutor police officer, we don't have that in the PCSOs, you just come in and you're teamed up with maybe an experienced PCSO, and we are just expected, whereas police officers have that tutor there who are trained and are getting paid a bit more to tutor that PC. But in the PCSO role we don't have that there; we are just expected to show other PCSOs what to do and how to do it. (PCSO Paul, Marshton)

As above with the shortcomings identified in the classroom training for PCSOs, the police organization has not invested the same level of resource for the field training for PCSOs as it does for police officers, reflecting the lower position PCSOs have within policing. While it is true that PCSOs do not have the same level of power, authority, and, therefore, responsibility that police officers do, they are often the main public face of policing in communities and will, by virtue of appearing to be a part of the police *team* (in dramaturgical terms), reflect poorly on the police service if they are not sufficiently confident in how to perform their role.

This lack of investment in PCSO training is also reflected in the 'refresher training' that these staff have during the course of their employment. As with police officers, PCSOs were expected to complete a degree of additional training to remind them of and to practice the skills they had been taught previously, and to introduce them to new developments, such as changes to their powers or the introduction of new technologies. There was a great deal of consistency here across the participants in terms of refresher training. Nearly every PCSO mentioned periodically attending courses in officer safety ('OST' or self-defence) and in first aid since their induction training. These courses were conducted in face-to-face classroom settings, but PCSOs also mentioned taking a range on online courses. These tended to cover topics such as changes in legislation, changes to the powers for PCSOs (which could happen when a new chief constable was appointed), issues of equality and diversity, and new technology systems being introduced.

While PCSOs appreciated these additional training opportunities, they did observe, however, that their range of refresher training was more limited than that offered to police officers. While they accepted that police officers, with their greater range of powers and authority compared with that of PCSOs, will have a greater need for additional training opportunities, the PCSOs felt that they would have also benefitted from periodic refresher training on their basic skills and powers. For example, PCSO Henry observes:

I think, to be honest, organisation needs to be looked at because police officers have what they call street skills training, and they get that once or twice a year. Now within that training, they refresh Bobbies on the powers, legislation, they throw scenarios at them, they deal with that scenario then they break it down, they analyze it so they can say 'well you should have done it this way as opposed to this way', or 'yes that was great'. PCSOs don't get that, and I think if organisation stepped up and gave us an ongoing PCSO street skills day, if you will, where they can train us and you go for a day's training and they'll spout 'well you can use this legislation, you can word it this way, you can use that'. You might never use that for another twelve months and then when it comes down to the one person that's says to you 'what is your power that you're acting on here, why are you doing this to me' and you're stood there are you're trying to think back twelve months and you're trying to think of the wording. What I'm trying to get at is if it's not refreshed every so often, it slips. So I think a lot of it, it comes down to an ongoing training issue. (PCSO Henry, Wellspring)

As Henry notes, while PCSOs do not have a wide range of power and authority, being members of support staff, they are the ones who spend the majority of their time in face-to-face encounters with members of the public and need to feel adequately prepared to handle these situations. Encounters with the public are unpredictable and without regular opportunities to be reminded of their powers and the activities in which they should be engaged, it is possible to stagnate, as PCSO Neive suggests:

I went on a course a couple of weeks ago, up-skilling, and the trainer asked how much service people had got and I was one of the longest serving, my friend was one of the first PCSOs and she's been doing it seven or eight years, and we have never had a training course regarding skills and refresher training as such. We get online training that we have to do but this is the first course that I went on that's new skills, new powers, and actually attending a course, and when asked for feedback we said 'every so may weeks police officers do street skills and they have a day's training', and it's like a refresher day, and I put that forward and said 'we should have the same, PCSOs should have the same' because it's like giving tickets out for public order. Some PCSOs do it a lot, some don't do it at all, some do it now and again, and if you don't do it, you lose it, and so they should refresh people's skills. (PCSO Neive, Wellspring)

Several of the PCSOs who, like Neive, had recently been trained on a new range of powers they were being granted by the recently appointed chief constable, found the sessions very helpful in terms of reminding them of the full extent of their existing powers and roles. However, the participants also mentioned that not all aspects of the PCSO role can be learned in the classroom or by a tutor in the field. For many, crucial elements of their work as a PCSO were learned 'on the job' in an informal way. The example of this cited most often was communication. For example, PCSO Tom describes how he can be asked to do a presentation with little warning:

I think it's a job you learn on the job. Nobody can teach you how to stand in front of a classroom of kids and talk, it's something that you can either do or you can't. Especially if you have to adlib, if somebody just says 'oh it's nice to see you outside the school, just come in and talk to the children', and you've not prepared anything, it's nice to be able to just go in and talk off the cuff as it was and be able to get your message across whatever the message is the school wants you to pass on. (PCSO Tom, Starrybridge)

For other PCSOs, a large part of their role involves being able to handle difficult situations or difficult people in a non-confrontational way. There are various routes to achieving this, some more orthodox than others, as PCSO Chris describes:

[T]raining didn't prepare you for actual engagement with people on the street as such. There was some parts of the training, I mean we did scenario based things, but that wasn't real life, you know. And there's a lot of bluff used you know, well I do, I use a lot of bluff because not everyone realises what we can and can't do, so using the right words in different situations, bluffing, you can put an end to the situation. (PCSO Chris, Hedgebourne)

Other PCSOs described how they would draw on their previous work and life experience when faced with challenging situations in the field. For example, PCSO Ellie (Fallhill) was employed by an airline before becoming a PCSO and had a great deal of experience with engaging angry and upset members of the public. PCSO Paul (Marston) had trained to be a teacher, and he used this background to facilitate communication with a wide range of community members. PCSOs are not alone in these observations that the real learning happens 'out there', as Fielding (1988) noted in his studies of police officer training and socialization processes (see also van Maanen 1975; Paoline 2003). The difference for PCSOs, however, is that this process of informal learning is often compounded by their earlier experiences of inadequate classroom training and brief shadowing periods, leaving them feeling inadequately equipped for their role. For example, PCSO Ellie (Fallhill) discovered that she needed to know how to handle evidence appropriately so as not to compromise it. However, as this was not something she had been formally taught, she had to ask a detective to show her how to do it. PCSO Alfie argued that the training downplays the inherent confrontational nature of the job, which means that PCSOs will have to learn in the field how to adapt to these situations within their limited range of powers. While it is true that a classroom environment and a divisional tutor will only ever be able to convey a portion of the reality of work as a PCSO (or police officer, Chan 2003), these officers have described a process which, intentionally or otherwise, falls short of what an organization could be reasonably expected to provide for its newest members.

Conclusion

This chapter has explored the different motivations which led the research participants to apply for work as a PCSO in their local police force. It has also considered the processes by which the police institution initiated these recruits into the organization and their early experiences in the field (the organizational socialization). This included formal classroom training, periods of shadowing their more experienced colleagues, periodic 'refresher' training on core skills, and the importance of informal learning. What has been evident from this discussion is not only the wide variability in terms of the length of the formal training aspects but also the consistency of view among many of the PCSOs that this training was either inadequate, inaccurate, or not realistic for the job that they now have. This puts added emphasis on the necessity of informal learning, either through the PCSOs' current or previous work experiences or by observing others. Van Maanen (1975) noted that the greater the separation of the recruit from the reality of their work in the socialization setting, the less they are able to generalize the skills they have learned there. Many of the PCSOs cited above had this exact experience, coupled with the knowledge that their role itself was still being questioned as legitimate by many of the officers they would be working alongside. (This will be further developed in Chapter 5.)

The outcome of these processes is that PCSOs are *institutionally undermined* by the organization which employs them. While PCSOs would not expect to have the same length and intensity of training which police officers receive, there was a consensus of view that the organization could have done more to prepare them for their work. What this suggests is that although PCSOs work for the police, are trained by them, and wear their uniform, they do not fully *belong* to the police at an organizational level. If we consider this in the dramaturgical sense, we can argue that the police have failed to equip their policing auxiliaries with the full range of performance tools which they need to give a convincing definition of the situation (as described in Chapter 3) during their interactions with members of the public and to present themselves as competent members of the policing team (Goffman 1959). The process of intuitionally undermining the PCSO performance began when the role was first created and introduced to police forces with little warning or time for preparation (Johnston 2005). Since then, however, the situation for PCSOs at the institutional level has not improved to a large degree. While some of the participants in this research have been employed as PCSOs since the role was new, and they would perhaps expect to encounter this lack of preparation in their initial training, newer recruits also discussed experiencing a lack of support and resourcing in their first few months in the organization. In addition, many of the PCSOs described how their ongoing training and development does not afford them the opportunity to refresh existing skills and responsibilities, as is the case for police officers. For a group of employees whose main role is to be the public face of the police in the local area, this lack of support, guidance, training, and development of their performance is surprising.

While the institutional processes which PCSOs experienced are important to consider, especially when discussing their early days in the organization, it is also important to examine the interpersonal socialization processes which they have experienced. These will include their interactions with police officers in their neighbourhood team, their supervisors, and their PCSO colleagues. It is to a dramaturgical analysis of these that we now turn because it will reveal in detail the nature of the pluralized police organization as these staff experience it.

5

Police Family Dynamics

While decisions made and processes run from an institutional level will have significant influence on Police Community Support Officers (PCSOs) in their workplace, their day-to-day encounters with other PCSOs and police officer colleagues are equally important to consider in order to understand fully PCSOs' experiences. The pluralized public police in England and Wales are often described as a police 'family' (Johnston 2005), as there are several members of this group, and each has a different role (such as police officers, PCSOs, and Special Constables). However, just how functional and harmonious a family this is will be shown to be variable between and within police forces. This chapter will consider the reasons for this from within a dramaturgical framework, in order to appreciate fully the nature and organization of these face-to-face interactions. This is similar to the work of Manning (1977), which is another example of dramaturgy applied to policing. In particular, Goffman's (1959) concepts of performances, teamwork, and regions will be used, and discrepant roles, communication out of character, and arts of impression management will be mentioned where appropriate. Unlike the previous chapter which examined institutional-level processes, Goffman's dramaturgical framework has been used directly to structure this chapter because it is central to an analysis of personal interaction within the neighbourhood policing teams (NPTs). Chapter 6 will then bring together the macro-level analysis from Chapter 4 and the micro-level analyses presented here to develop a picture of occupational culture within pluralized public policing.

The chapter has three main sections. The first discusses performances, through which the actions PCSOs take to present a compelling definition of the situation (as described in Chapter 3) and their competency as actors are illustrated. The second section focuses on teamwork, and it shows how PCSOs and police officers

Police Community Support Officers. First Edition. Megan O'Neill. © Megan O'Neill 2019. Published 2019 by Oxford University Press.

operate as separate, yet connected, performance teams. The final section explores the regions in which interaction within the pluralized policing field takes place, and how this reveals the nature and structure of PCSO and police officer relationships. As in previous chapters, the data to be utilized here come from the six NPTs observed during the course of the research: Fallhill, Marshton, and Starrybridge from the Northport Police Force, and Hedgebourne, Wellspring, and Fayhaven from the Aldhamshire Police Force.

Performances

For PCSOs in the company of their police officer colleagues, conveying a believable performance to police officers that PCSOs are equal and competent members of the team is an ongoing and daily effort. Many PCSOs reported that the initial scepticism (and sometimes open hostility) which followed the development of the PCSO role (e.g. BBC 2006; see also Caless 2007) has never entirely disappeared from the police service in England and Wales. Although PCSOs from all six NPTs reported this experience, it was a more regular occurrence for the Fayhaven and Marshton PCSOs than for the Starrybridge, Hedgebourne, and Fallhill PCSOs.[1] The main focus of a PCSO's performance was, therefore, to demonstrate to police constables (PCs) both their usefulness and ability in their role, even if the PCSO in question had by this point become disillusioned with it because of the lack of promotion and often routine nature of the work (i.e. a 'Cynical' performer—see Cosgrove 2011). The research revealed that some NPTs had a greater level of acceptance and integration of PCSOs than others. For example, as PCSOs in Starrybridge enjoyed amicable relationships with the police officers in their teams, the art of managing their performance front was easier. Convincing their audience (PCs) that they are competent and worthy colleagues was not as difficult as it was for those who did not have close relationships with police officers in the NPT, such as was the case for the Fayhaven PCSOs. The following PCSO describes how over time, many police officers have become more

[1] PCSOs in Wellspring worked in a station with very few police officers present, so the nature of the interaction between these groups in this area is difficult to assess.

accepting of PCSOs, especially when they can demonstrate their usefulness to officers:

MO: So do you feel like you get along with your police officer colleagues here?
I do here, no problem. I socialise, we are friends, we socialise with families. Some of them will tell you straight, they don't believe in the role of a PCSO, but it's the person as well who makes the role […] but on the same sheet, my neighbourhood manager (NM) is Ethan and he's told me that sometimes he will come in to do a job and there's nothing left for him to do because we have done it, so that gives him the opportunity then to either spend a bit more time on an investigation or just go and do what an NM does which is again, is along the role of a PCSO where you can get into the schools and stuff like that. (PCSO Tom, Starrybridge)

This view is supported by PC Beth, who felt that PCSOs are well integrated in their NPT, although she was not convinced of the need for PCSOs when she first joined neighbourhood policing:

MO: How did you feel when PCSOs were first introduced, did it register with you at first?
Until I came here which was about three years ago, I'd say I had a negative view which I think a lot of PCs who haven't worked with PCSOs think that. I used to work in the Tactical Aid Unit as well, the riot police. So quite a distant department from what I do here, and I'd say your outlook on them would be what's the point of having them? You don't know what they do but you could say that about many roles within the police. There's a lack of understanding between different departments and you think the next department does nothing. So yes, once I came here, and you start working alongside and seeing the work that they do, then you realise that they are valuable. (PC Beth, Fallhill)

PCSOs in Starrybridge, Hedgebourne, and Fallhill have largely succeeded in demonstrating their 'usefulness' to their police officer colleagues. This, however, is not always the experience of PCSOs, such as Jeffery from Fayhaven (below). In his experience, PCs are not as supportive here as in places such as Starrybridge, even with PCSOs being well-established in the NPT. He uses the example of unsolicited assistance to demonstrate:

Sometimes they'll drive past you and offer you a lift somewhere, but that's probably as much as it goes. Unless you go and specifically ask them for some support or advice or something, they'll not necessarily freely give it to you, if you like, they'll not approach you and say 'do you need any help', they'll wait for you to go to them and say 'can you help me with this'. (PCSO Jeffery, Fayhaven)

PCSO Alfie discusses how the initial recruitment process for PCSOs left a very difficult legacy in terms of ongoing relationships between PCs and PCSOs, one against which PCSOs have to struggle.

MO: When PCSOs were first introduced, some police officers weren't very enthusiastic about the idea. Do you feel that that has changed at all? I think it has changed. I think, initially, there was a lot of skepticism about the role, then I think PCs might not necessarily felt threatened by PCSOs but they knew that with the introduction of PCSOs, that meant there was going to be less PCs. […] And as I mentioned to you before, I think when PCSOs had the major drive for the recruitment, […] rather than get the best people for the job, they just had to fill those positions and maybe got people who didn't do our reputation any good whatsoever, which I think set us back quite a lot with the media, the public, and also PCs because PCs come into regular contact with the people that maybe were recruited as a result of being a numbers exercise rather than a capability exercise. […] It has been mentioned that the PCSO assessment centre was held in a disco and they just shouted 'anybody who wants to be a PCSO put your hands up'. But it's one of those things, PCs were always going to ridicule our role to a degree because we don't have the powers that they've got but that's because it's a different role and I think a lot of them failed to recognise that we actually take away a lot of the rubbish jobs that they don't want to do, but they very quickly forget that. (PCSO Alfie, Fayhaven)

As PCSOs have a shorter training period and less enforcement power than PCs do, they must constantly strive to convey to police officers that they are performing a believable role as valuable and supportive NPT members. This aspect of their performance front, that of being a PCSO, will compromise their performances to varying degrees, depending on the NPT in which they work. PCSOs in Starrybridge, Hedgebourne, and Fallhill did not find this to be as much of a constant challenge as did the Fayhaven and Marston PCSOs, who were not fully accepted by police officer colleagues.

For many PCSOs, the most direct way to convey successfully a performance of equal competence to other members of the NPT is to demonstrate their usefulness in criminal investigation through gathering information on residents in the local area of interest to the police (Cosgrove and Ramshaw 2013). Being adept at communicating with, engaging with, and reassuring community members, the primary focus of the PCSO role (ACPO 2007) is not sufficient for demonstrating a believable performance when interacting with some police officers in the NPT, as this PC from Marshton demonstrates:

MO: So what makes for a bad PCSO?

Bad PCSOs will not know what's going on in their area, don't know who people are, will spend a lot of time signing in problems, will spend a lot of time sat in places having cups of tea and not actually doing work. They never stop people and ask what they're doing, customer account forms, that kind of stuff. They very rarely see people, not doing what they're getting paid to do. They get away with as much as they can, I think. And like I said people that work really hard are getting tarnished with that brush which is unfair. (PC Stuart, Marshton)

For this and many other PCs, a 'good' PCSO is one who can gather a great deal of reliable information on the local area, or 'intelligence', which is brought back to the station and passed on to police colleagues to assist in criminal investigations, an activity traditionally valued by police officers (Reiner 2010; Cosgrove and Ramshaw 2013). Some PCSOs reported to me that for them, being 'sat in places having cups of tea' was viewed as community engagement (if those cups of tea were had in public places—a topic developed below, in the section discussing regions) as they were making themselves available to members of the community for an informal chat and generally being visible. This, however, is clearly not an effective way to convey a 'definition of the situation', where they are active and competent members of the NPT to police colleagues, especially in areas like Fayhaven and Marshton, where relationships between PCs and PCSOs were sometimes difficult.

To counter this effect, PCSOs may attend to 'dramatic realization' (Goffman 1959; Manning 1977), whereby they highlight aspects of their work which are more acceptable to police colleagues, and convey the type of performance which police officers value. This will entail actions such as widely disseminating internally information which they have gathered on a key suspect from the local area, talking with colleagues in the breakroom or kitchen about a dramatic encounter which they had while on patrol (which they dealt with themselves), or, more generally, going beyond their role, such as setting up a rural crime-watch scheme.

This mirrors the tendency of police officers to engage in 'storytelling', as noted by earlier police culture researchers (see e.g. Waddington 1999; Shearing and Ericson 1991; van Hulst 2013), to highlight the more dramatic aspects of their work. For the PCSOs in Starrybridge, Hedgebourne, and Fallhill, this technique was generally successful because their police officer colleagues were more willing to believe these performances because of their close working relationships. See the following example of dramatic realization in Starrybridge:

PCSO Tom came into the common room with a load of Post Office bags and enthusiastically told us all the story (me, PCSO Charlie and two PCs). An offender seems to have stolen a bag of large post items from a Royal Mail van at the local post office. He then went inside the post office and asked for some carrier bags. He took the contents of post bags, put them in the carrier bags and left the post bags at the scene. PCSO Tom responded to get a statement and collected the post bags. It is a 'negative lines' (no solid evidence and no suspects) crime now, but that might change. Tom is chasing up council CCTV and bus CCTV, following up leads from the post office and the dentist (the offender had been at the dentist before going to the post office). The PCs in the room were intrigued by the story and offered suggestions for other ways to obtain possible evidence. (Field notes 12/12, Starrybridge)

The PCSOs in Fayhaven, Marshton, and Wellspring, however, were starting from a lower point of integration in the team, and thus dramatic realization was more difficult to achieve, often because PCs and PCSOs in this station tended to avoid being in the station at the same time (see the section below on regions). Thus there were few opportunities to regale success stories or verbally share intelligence which PCSOs had gathered. Even if there were such opportunities, the PCSOs and PCs usually worked separately and tended not to explore ways to collaborate very often.

Successfully conveying performances of competence, usefulness, and value to police colleagues is a craft which PCSOs undertake daily through a variety of strategies, such as gathering useful information on the community, being able to look after themselves in physical confrontations, and assisting in arrests. All of these relate to enforcement work, which was intended to be a lesser part of the PCSO role, but which the research suggests is more highly valued by police officers, and fits with the cultural preference for action (Holdaway 1983). While regularly maintaining these types of performances can take significant effort, PCSOs do not do this in isolation from each other. As will be discussed next, Goffman conceives of performances as the work of a 'team', even when a person is performing in that moment on his or her own. Every PCSO, to some degree, represents the totality of PCSOs in that NPT.

Teamwork

During the course of the observational research presented here, it became clear that PCSOs work as a single performance team, separate from that of PCs. This can be evidenced through the following three elements to be discussed below: (i) PCSO training, (ii) how PCSOs avoid spoiling the team performance, and (iii) their relationships with PCs.

Training

The previous chapter on becoming a PCSO mentioned how 'shadowing' is a component of PCSO training. In order to learn the details of the performance which PCSOs will be conveying, it is important for new recruits to the PCSO role to have an opportunity to observe their teammates before they attempt the job on their own. While many PCSOs felt it was helpful to observe PCs, as well, they did not get a full sense of their role as a PCSO until they had observed a fellow PCSO. For example, PCSO Deborah describes her early experiences:

MO: So you didn't shadow an existing PCSO?

No, it was a police officer. So you did feel safe and then we all got sent onto our teams […] I got put onto my new team then, and then Jessica (a PCSO) took me under her wing, and she was like 'come on, I'll show you how it's done'. So I was quite fortunate really because I shadowed her for a couple of weeks and then gained more confidence and then I was fine going out eventually. But people do need to be in company with someone for quite a while I think, because some days you can come across nothing, which you've probably experienced. And then other days it can be absolutely mental and overwhelming. So yes, I think you do need to be with someone for a while, definitely.

MO: So she wasn't tasked to mentor you, she just did it on her own?

No. Yes, she was nice to enough to say 'come on, I'll take you out', so that was nice really, and that made me feel welcomed when I went onto the group. (PCSO Deborah, Marshton)

This PCSO did not feel fully ready for the role and integrated into the team until she had an opportunity to be mentored by an existing and experienced PCSO. Careful supervision by a PC, trained to tutor PCSOs (as Deborah's was), is not sufficient to learn fully the PCSO performance, which suggests PCs are not members of PCSOs' performance team. However, as PCSO Paul (Marshton) warned in Chapter 3, there also needs to be a degree of training and investment in the PCSO mentor in order to make the role meaningful and effective. PCs who tutor PCSOs are paid for this additional role, whereas PCSOs who act as mentors are not. This again reflects the separation of the teams, although more from an organizational level, in that there is a dedicated and paid position for PC tutors, whereas the same arrangement is not in place for PCSOs. The beat tutoring phase appears to be a crucial component of training, for both PCs and PCSOs, and one which reflects the place PCSOs hold within the organization owing to this lack of investment.

Spoiling a performance

As Goffman has argued, only true teammates have the power to 'give the show away or to disrupt it by inappropriate conduct' (1990: 88). Careful attention to detail is needed to convey the best performance possible. The following field note describes a scene where a less experienced PCSO is learning some of this detail.

PCSO Trudy is not as familiar with the smartphones or the radio yet. She works part time and so doesn't get as much practice in as the other staff. She was teased recently about not using the phonetic alphabet on the radio. Today when we were in the car, PCSO Alfie was advising her on how to close off the job on the smartphone. Earlier during the meal break with other PCSOs when she wasn't there, Alfie joked about her and said she has one day on and 12 days off. (Field notes 7/03, Fayhaven)

This field note is interesting on two levels. For the first, we can see one PCSO helping another, less experienced PCSO to learn the mechanics of the equipment in private, away from the public or police officers. This was especially important in areas like Fayhaven and Marshton, where relationships with police officers were not at amicable as they were in Starrybridge, Fallhill, or Hedgebourne. This gives her a safe environment to both perfect her performance and appear competent in front of PCs, thus illustrating two of

Goffman's 'arts of impression management': dramaturgical discipline and circumspection (Goffman 1990: 210–12). Through these processes, performers control the impression that they give to those outside the group and the steps they can take to control and perfect that performance. The second level relates to the way this PCSO was teased when she was not present (although she was also teased directly). This sends out a clear message to other PCSOs about the approved way to conduct the PCSO performance, i.e. full time, with complete competence (as was discussed in the earlier section on performances). As was usual for meal breaks in Fayhaven, no PCs were present, and thus the overall PCSO performance was not compromised with this teasing (more on this below). Other PCSOs spoke more explicitly of how fellow PCSOs can let the team down by their behaviour.

What affects me most in this job, what I don't like, and it's very bitter this but I don't like the fact of other people's sick leave records [...] With this job you've got a lot of other people that can do your job, but you still hold your own responsibilities and I feel that some people do take the mick out of their sick leave, and I don't like the fact that they're off for months at a time [...] That really upsets me [...] I can walk round the streets and the public can say to me 'why haven't I seen such a body', and some people don't even know some PCSOs that cover their area. (PCSO Charlie, Starrybridge)

For Charlie, chronically absent colleagues are disruptive not so much because of the increased workload for other PCSOs, but because it conveys a bad impression to outsiders. In Goffman's analysis, only performance team members can have this sort of impact. Were his other PCSO colleagues not a part of Charlie's performance team, their absence would not be as significant for him.

Correcting the performances of teammates in private is another key example of how PCSOs are part of the same performance team. I observed on several occasions how PCSOs working in pairs would support each other's decisions in front of outsiders, but then challenge or chastise each other when in private so as to preserve the outward performance, as the following field note from Wellspring demonstrates:

We then encountered a van going the wrong way up a one way road. PCSO Henry flashed the head lights but the van went past us. We turned round, Henry flashed the lights again and the van stopped. The PCSOs got the driver's details and checked him out on their smartphones while chatting to him. They gave him a warning: 'You are lucky tonight because I'm on my way home,' said Henry. The implication was that otherwise the sanction would have been worse, which isn't really true. Back in the car, PCSO Neive asked, 'what would you have done if he'd challenged you? We can't ticket for that.' Henry said, 'Anti-social use of motor vehicle.' Neive said, 'That's shaky ground!' Henry: 'I've done it before!' This was all said in a friendly, teasing sort of way. (Field note 18/02, Wellspring)

PCSO Neive was careful not to challenge her colleague openly in front of people who are outside of their performance team, as this would spoil their collective performance. As Goffman (1959) discusses, correcting a mistake a performer has made in front of an audience only serves to deepen the performer's transgression, as it lets the audience into knowledge usually reserved for teammates. Normally, teammates avoid doing this in public and save these sorts of conversations for private moments. This is part of what Goffman refers to as 'audience segregation' (1990: 137): keeping control of which performance an audience sees. It also supports another of the arts of impression management: dramaturgical loyalty, in which performers offer each other moral support in the face of a common audience (Goffman 1990: 207). In all of the cases above, PCs are conspicuous by their absence. The nature of direct interaction between PCSOs and PCs is discussed next.

Relationships with police constables

A final demonstration that PCSOs are part of the same performance team and PCs are outside of this team can be achieved by examining relationships between PCs and PCSOs in front of members of the public. There were several occasions where PCSOs conveyed experiences of being ignored or ridiculed by police officers when away from the public, such as in the police station. As discussed above, PCSOs do still struggle at times to be accepted by police officers. However, to be openly chastised by a police officer in public is a clear demonstration that the PC and the PCSO are not part of the same performance team, as this field note demonstrates:

PCSO Henry drove me to a bus stop closer to my home in his own car at the end of the shift. On the way he told me a story about a PC in the office where he used to work who acts like a law unto himself. This PC once complained about PCSOs in front of Henry and a member of the public. Henry told him off in private later. He would never say such things about PCs to a member of the public. (Field note 25/02, Wellspring)

As we can see, being publicly chastised is out with the boundaries of the performance team. Teammates do not do this, even when a colleague has let them down in some way. Earlier quotes from PCSOs in Fayhaven and Starrybridge discuss how PCSOs can put in a poor performance, but these grievances are not aired in front of outsiders in order to preserve the overall team performance of competence and usefulness. The PC above was clearly not worried about his performance as a police officer being put at risk with a member of the public having a poor impression of his PCSO colleague.

This is mirrored in an exchange I had with PC Peter when he and I were arranging a day and time to do an interview. The inspector had suggested, in front of this PC, that I speak to Peter as he regularly works with PCSOs. Normally I would decide for myself whom to ask for an interview or take suggestions from sergeants or inspectors away from the PCs. Thus this PC and I were in effect put in a position of being unable to say no. This perhaps explains the following remark the PC made, within earshot of the entire NPT, including PCSOs:

PC Peter: 'So you want to know what I think about PCSOs? I can tell you that now! Wankers!' (Field note 28/01, Hedgebourne)

While I was not a usual member of the public in that I had access to the backstage areas for PCs and PCSOs, I was not a member of any of their performance teams, either, which makes me an audience. This open derision of PCSOs, while partially in jest, does reflect a clear boundary between the groups in that fostering a negative view of PCSOs in an audience member does not have a similar negative implication for police officers.

As members of the same police service, PCs have access to internal information on PCSOs and their performances, which can spoil the PCSO performance when in public, as demonstrated in the quotes above. This does not mean, however, that they are part of the same performance team. As Goffman argues, 'the individuals who are on the staff of an establishment are not members of a team by virtue of their staff status, but only by virtue of the cooperation which they maintain in order to sustain a given definition of the situation' (1990: 108). PCSOs work together to present themselves as competent and valuable members of a performance team, which is a part of the overall NPT (as presented in Chapter 3). However, other members of the NPT and other police officers are not co-performers with PCSOs but one of the audiences to whom they perform. This makes them performance 'colleagues' in Goffman's terms (1990: 159), not members of the same performance team. While PCs do have the power to discredit the PCSO performance when out in public as they have a good deal of internal group information, they are not themselves members of the PCSO performance team. Criticism from police officers when *inside* the police station, while upsetting, is not very damaging because it is not coming from within the PCSO team. It in fact has the tendency to bind PCSOs closer together as a performance team as it is one of the definitions of the situation which they regularly work against in their performances and which perpetuates the 'us-versus-them' (i.e. us within the team against those outside it) atmosphere described by several PCSOs during the course of the research, especially in areas like Fayhaven and Marshton. How PCSOs are trained when on the beat, learning the team's performances and skills, and their relationships with PCs as discussed in this section on teamwork, all point towards PCSOs and PCs occupying separate performance teams. This will be further developed in next section on regions.

Regions

This last analytical section will examine the physical spaces that the PCSO performance teams use, which will further demonstrate their separate team status from that of their police officer colleagues, as well as highlight the nature of their relationships with police officers. The section above mentioned a few examples from the fieldwork where PCSOs corrected each other's performances in private spaces, away from the gaze of those not a part of that performance, such as in the car or in the breakroom in Fayhaven. For PCSOs, many of the elements of the frontstage and backstage, as described by Goffman (1959), hold true. The frontstage is the space where performances are enacted for an audience and where performance team members try to present the best and most convincing role that they can, keeping at bay any conflicting or discrediting information. Backstages are the areas where the performance can be contradicted or rehearsed, or in which it is prepared. Performance team members will knowingly contradict their performances in the backstage regions as long as they are safe from the gaze of the audience. As was discussed above, PCSOs in Fayhaven and Wellspring used the police car (one of their usual backstages) to demonstrate to each other how to use the radios and smartphones or to challenge each other's behaviour from when they previously had been in front of outsiders to the team (such as the public or PCs). The backstage regions for PCSOs also include certain spaces in the police station. This backstage will be discussed in more detail below, mainly with reference to field notes taken when with PCSOs in these spaces.

The police station is a complex backstage. Some elements of it are open to the public (mainly the front desk) and are thus a frontstage, some elements are backstage, for both police officers and PCSOs, and some elements are backstage for PCSOs alone, away from all other police officers. How PCSOs navigate these complex arrangements for relaxing and perfecting their performance is illustrative of the nature of their relationships with police officers, as well as that of the architecture of the building itself. Wooff and Skinns (2017) in their study of police custody suites show how the structure of police spaces can determine social practice within it, as well as personal experiences. This is also the case for PCSOs in police stations and in cars, in that these varied from one area to another. As with the examples given above about the police car being a backstage where performances could be perfected, so too is the NPT's office. This was the case for Fallhill, Starrybridge, Fayhaven, and Wellspring. This is the space where PCs and PCSOs use shared computers to do their online paperwork and e-mails, and it is usually where the radio chargers and the team's telephones (both landline and chargers for the mobiles) are located. Even though there is often a locker room nearby, many members of the NPT will put on their policing gear (besides the uniform) in this communal area: vests, radio, equipment belts, coats, etc. There were several occasions of PCSOs asking each other to check that they had done this correctly, and to adjust anything that was out of place. PCs will also conduct these final performance-perfecting tasks in the office area, thus both performance teams (PCs and PCSOs) will use this space for the same backstage purpose. In contrast, for Marston and Hedgebourne, the NPT's office was a large, open-plan space which was shared with other policing teams. This prevented it from being used as an area (a backstage) where performers could manage their performance 'front', as, in effect, it had become a frontstage because of the presence of other teams. The usual rituals of collecting and putting on equipment tended to be done in the locker rooms. The following field note extract from Hedgebourne shows how the presence of an inspector can reinforce the frontstage nature of the office:

PCSO Layla and a PC said that the Inspector is cracking the whip about standards, people sitting and chatting in the office, etc. The Inspector wants people to go out straight away [...] The Inspector is upset about dress, hair, nails, people sitting around. They need to have a valid reason for sitting in the station. There is also whip cracking about swearing (in front of me?). Swearing is not professional. PCSO Layla said I should deny it if I hear anything - don't get yourself involved as a witness! (Field note 28/01, Hedgebourne)

This concern about standards and behaviour from the inspector means that whenever he was around, the officers and staff needed to perform a certain way. This meant that the NPT office, which in some police stations was a backstage, was often a frontstage for these PCs and PCSOs (van Hulst 2017). This reflects a degree of 'communication out of character' (Goffman 1959) in that PCs and PCSOs would temporarily act in collusion when the senior officer was present in order to present the office as more ordered than it had been when he was not there. This is an example of 're-aligning actions' (Goffman 1959) between two separate performance teams who would normally perform for each other, but who, in that moment, were performing with each other for the benefit of a common audience (the inspector).

Although many of the backstages are shared between PCs and PCSOs, a clear difference occurs in the breakroom where PCs and PCSOs take their meals. In Starrybridge, for example, the breakroom was a large space with sofas and a television, along with a table, chairs, and kitchen units. PCs and PCSOs would use this room together and clearly enjoyed each other's company while taking their meal breaks. This suggests that PCSOs could relax in this shared backstage area, even with PCs present. The situation was very different in Fayhaven. The kitchen was a small, galley-style space with no room for a table or chairs. The one large conference room in the station also doubled as a breakroom. However, PCSOs and PCs tended to use this space at different times, with PCSOs often co-ordinating their meal breaks to all eat together, without PCs present. There seemed to be an unspoken arrangement where if the breakroom was being used by PCSOs, the PCs would come back later or take their meals elsewhere. The PCSOs thereby created a space where they could be at ease, away from PCs. This clearly signified who was a part of this performance team and who was not—PCs serve as an audience for the PCSO performance team in Fayhaven and Marston and so are kept away from this backstage region during breaks as much as possible (Goffman 1959). The spatial situation in Marston was somewhat different from other NPTs in that the breakroom was more a traditional canteen, where staff from across the building would meet to eat together. While there was no food service here, there were kitchen units, refrigerators, vending machines, and several rows of tables and chairs. Some PCSOs opted to avoid this room entirely and would meet together in old police stations (closed to the public) in their beat areas instead, at predetermined times. This meant not only that they did not have to travel a distance to get back to the breakroom but also that they could be completely at ease during their break, knowing that there were no police officers nearby.

Even in stations such as Starrybridge, Fallhill, and Hedgebourne, where PCs and PCSOs are able to relax together in the backstage areas, there is still an important difference between these teams in terms of the degree to which each can relax. PCSOs as members of staff are allowed to take a certain amount of uninterrupted time each day for unpaid tea breaks and meals. During these periods, they radio into the control room that they will be unavailable. This is not the case for PCs, who can be called to 'jobs' at any time and must respond, even if taking one of their paid breaks. Some PCSOs (although not all) turn their radios off during breaks. This is never an option to PCs, who are always 'on duty', even at meal times. Thus, the backstage for PCs is far less permanent or certain than it is for PCSOs.

Outside of break times, some PCSOs find it difficult to be completely at ease in the police station whenever police officers are around. For example, in Marshton, most of the NPT is located in two, large, open-plan offices. One of these offices holds a large computer display screen on one wall, which shows the location of every PCSO and PC on the team, by using a tracking signal through their radios. This sent a clear message to PCSO Steve:

> That's our mapping system so they can see where everybody is. So when we were told to go to [Area C] yesterday, if I would have said 'ah there's loads [of PCSOs] there, sod it, we will go back to [Area A]', they would see that I hadn't been there. You can probably get in a bit more trouble. (PCSO Steve, Marshton)

This tracking system makes it clear that even when PCSOs are out on their beats, they are still being tracked for compliance with supervisors' instructions. Even potential backstages are compromised in this method if too many PCSOs are tracked in the same location for an extended period. Whenever possible, PCSOs in Marshton would congregate in a small office down the corridor from the large ones which held a computer and a desk. This seemed to be an area reserved for PCSOs, and they could hold private conversations there out of earshot of PCs or supervisors. This seemed to be the space in which they could be most relaxed when in the station. When the PCSOs were not in the smaller room together, they could still manage to signal each other in the large open-plan office through knowing looks and glances across the room. This is more 'communication out of character' (Goffman 1959) in that it was a way of exchanging information between teammates that would not normally be done in front of an audience but was subtle enough for the PCs not to notice.

By considering the use of space, specifically the frontstage and backstage regions of interaction used by PCSOs and PCs, we can achieve a clear sense of the boundaries between these two performance teams. In cases where PCs and PCSOs are on good terms and will eat and socialize together, such as in Starrybridge, Fallhill, and Hedgebourne, there is still a difference in relation to how permanent a backstage the breakroom is for each team. PCSOs can be completely off duty at these times, whereas PCs cannot. In those NPTs where PCSOs and PCs do not get along well, such as in Fayhaven or Marshton, this is reflected in their use of space in the station: PCSOs taking separate meal breaks or finding quiet areas away from PCs in which to congregate with other PCSOs. Although PCs and PCSOs comprise separate performance teams, as has been demonstrated in the sections above on *Performances, Teamwork* and this section on *Regions*, the extent to which these teams are willing to work together to give a consistent performance to members of the public (an audience for both of them, outside of their organization) will vary. This is further developed in the conclusion.

Conclusion

While they may be configured as one team (the NPT) in the operational sense, this analysis has shown that PCSOs and PCs comprise two separate teams in the dramaturgical sense. PCSOs in particular work together to present a unified definition of the situation (that of being competent and useful members of the NPT, as was explored in Chapter 3). They do not challenge each other in front of their audiences and they use the backstage regions to perfect their appearances and to relax—often away from police officers. In some cases, the community police officers have good relationships with PCSOs and the boundaries between these two performance teams will be much less pronounced. These PCs and PCSOs will eat and socialize together, will support each other when in public, and, in general, work together throughout the day to convey a generalized police 'front' to local residents.

As discussed in the section on teamwork, while Goffman did acknowledge that staff members of a particular organization may have insider knowledge of each other's performances, this does not by itself mean that they are members of the same performance team (Goffman 1959), only that they are part of the same occupational group, or 'colleagues', as he referred to it. This group will be comprised of several performance teams, although this may not be apparent to those outside of the organization (e.g. members of the public). I would like to develop Goffman's discussion of groups further. In the case of PCs and PCSOs, some NPTs (the 'group') had performance teams which worked well together—what I will call *complementary teams*. These were NPTs such as Starrybridge, Fallhill, and Hedgebourne. In other NPTs, PCSOs and PCs worked less closely and, in one case, hardly at all. In these groups, the performance teams are what I will call *competitive teams*. These would be NPTs such as Fayhaven and Marshton. In the main, PCSOs in NPTs with complementary performance teams appeared to be more satisfied with their work, PCs and PCSOs shared information about people and incidents with each other freely and shared the NPT resources willingly. In the NPTs with competitive teams, PCSOs seemed less satisfied in their work, could feel defensive around PCs, and did not often collaborate with PCs or other police colleagues. These teams related to each other in a competitive way in that the resources of the NPT (e.g. computers, the breakroom, or the patrol car) were not willingly shared, intelligence from PCSOs may not be passed on as fully as it could have been (e.g. only via the database but without direct discussion or collaboration with the PC concerned), and, as there is finite funding for neighbourhood policing, some PCs would regard PCSOs as competition for wages, i.e. that there are fewer PCs than there could be if PCSOs did not exist (see e.g. Muir 2010). In the complementary teams, this was not much of an issue, as the work of PCSOs was generally valued. While this demarcation of the performance teams into complementary and competitive is similar to that of Bott's (1957) analysis of 'joint' and 'segregated' conjugal teams, the element of competition here is a marked difference.

What this demarcation of performance teams into competitive and complementary structures points to is a more nuanced and pluralized arrangement for those who are the public face of policing in England and Wales, those who might be considered the 'street cops', than is reflected in some other analyses, such as that of Reuss-Ianni (1983). While it is true that even competitive teams, such as those in Marshton, will collude to present an agreed definition of the situation to a common audience, such as a supervisor, they are not a unified group of performers. While the different role, powers, and degree of training for each performance team is an element of their segregation, it is not deterministic of their interactions. Areas such as Starrybridge, Fallhill, and Hedgebourne demonstrated complementary and collaborative working arrangements between PCs and PCSOs, despite these differences, whereas Marshton and Fayhaven did not. This suggests that the internal cultural divisions of public policing are variable, and they fluctuate depending on local circumstances and management choices, and do not align to rank or role alone. This discussion of policing culture, including the role of managers within it, will be developed further in Chapter 6.

This chapter and Chapter 4 have explored not only the process of joining the police service as a PCSO, but also that of *becoming* a PCSO and defending the definition of the situation (the ideal PCSO performance), which was described in Chapter 3. By going through the stages of applying, training, and integrating into a

NPT, PCSOs learn not only 'the ropes' but also their *place* in the organization. As this discussion has shown, what that place is will vary from one NPT to another in terms of how collaborative relationships are with police officers. The common feature, however, is that PCSOs and PCs do not work as teammates in a dramaturgical sense, but as separate performance teams. It terms of learning one's place, this is an early and at times harsh lesson for PCSOs. This arrangement is due to a number of factors, not just the inherent differential nature of the roles, but also in relation to the degree to which the policing organization supports and invests in its PCSOs (the extent to which PCSOs are institutionally undermined), and in relation to the local occupational cultural configurations of the NPT (whether the performance teams are complementary or competitive). Thus Chapters 3–5 have considered what PCSOs do, how they become embedded in the organization, and what interaction is like with others in policing. The next section of the book, Part III, will analyse these findings in terms of what implications they have for the police culture literature, as well as what implications they have for the changing face of community policing in the UK and beyond.

PART III

Analysis

6

Police Community Support Officer Culture in a Pluralized Field

This penultimate chapter of the book will bring together the research described so far and analyse its significance for an understanding of the occupational culture of Police Community Support Officers (PCSOs) within the pluralized field of public policing. Existing studies of police occupational culture were described in Chapter 1, and these have indeed produced useful insights over the years as to how the police address their common 'predicament' (Reiner 2010: 137), albeit faced in different contexts and at different points in time. While PCSOs do not have the same powers and responsibilities as police constables (PCs), they too have an occupational culture which is shaped, to a degree, by similar experiences and challenges to those of police officers (Cosgrove 2015). Both groups are uniformed representatives of the state with a degree of authority over its citizens, who are expected to be highly visible and solve local problems related to crime and safety. These occupational circumstances will generate particular responses, although, as will be argued, the responses of PCSOs have produced notable variations from those of police officers. It is therefore relevant to draw upon the existing cannon of literature to inform the following analysis. However, this analysis of the occupational culture for PCSOs will present challenges to some of the existing theories of police occupational culture in general, and thus the results will have implications for future analyses of the pluralized policing field and its occupational cultures both in the UK and more widely.

Chapter 4 examined the processes by which the research participants decided to become PCSOs and were introduced to the organization, and it demonstrated an unspoken but evident system of 'institutional undermining' of the PCSO role. This system operated at the macro-level of the organization, and while some elements of

Police Community Support Officers. First Edition. Megan O'Neill. © Megan O'Neill 2019. Published 2019 by Oxford University Press.

the system may not have been deliberately or consciously enacted, the overall result was one identified by many of the participants: a sense that the police organization was not fundamentally orientated towards their wellbeing and professional development and that, at times, these staff had to struggle to attain the basic support and resources readily offered to police officers. Chapter 5, in contrast, took a micro-level perspective to understand the nature and structure of the relationships between PCSOs and their police officer colleagues. Chapter 5 used Goffman's (1959) dramaturgical perspective to illustrate how the two groups (PCs and PCSOs) operate as separate performance teams, rather than as one unified one. It further argued that the relationships between these teams varied in that in some areas the teams worked in a 'complementary' way while in others the relationship was 'competitive'.

In this chapter, these two phenomena of institutional undermining and complementary/competitive teams will be brought together through the framework developed by Chan (1997) to analyse police and PCSO culture in a pluralized public policing field. This will highlight the processes of developing and enacting an occupational culture through storytelling and its artefacts (two distinct aspects of occupational culture which are often conflated). The chapter will explore how these processes and artefacts—while appearing similar to those of police officers—have significant variations for PCSOs, in comparison to police officers, and these reveal their unique occupational culture.

Chan and *Changing Police Culture*

One of the most influential analyses of police occupational culture in recent times is that of Janet Chan (1996, 1997, 2003, and 2007). Chan's research of failed cultural change in an Australian police force in the face of high-profile accusations of institutional racism generated a strong response (both positive and negative), and it continues to influence police culture scholarship to this day (O'Neill 2016). Chan built her theoretical framework from the amalgamation of several existing texts, in particular, that of Bourdieu (Bourdieu and Wacquant 1992; Sackmann 1991; Shearing and Ericson 1991). Chan (1997) argues that much of the existing literature on police culture takes a linear view of the process by which culture is generated in an organization and is adopted by its members. Instead of regarding culture as something that officers accept without question and blindly use to guide practice, she argues instead for a more dynamic model. Chan (1997) places the police officer at the centre of the process which has three main factors. Bourdieu's concepts of 'field' and 'habitus' (Bourdieu and Wacquant 1992) are used to describe, respectively, the wider structural and political forces within policing generally (structural positions) and the personal orientations and interpretations of the officer individually (cultural dispositions). The third factor is police practice itself. In Chan's model, the police officer influences and is influenced by all three factors so that none of them is completely deterministic of the other.

For the purposes of this chapter, it is useful to explore the concept of 'habitus' in more detail, as it is here where police occupational culture is constructed and actioned. Bourdieu presents habitus as a series of dispositions, or 'a feel for the game'. This enables a person to cope with unexpected situations which may emerge from an encounter with a particular field, such as policing (Bourdieu and Wacquant 1992). Individuals in these situations will draw on their previous experiences and their knowledge of the range of 'moves' open to them in this game when deciding what course of action to take. This is similar to Sackmann's (1991) concept of cultural knowledge in organizations. For Chan (1997), Sackmann (1991) presents a useful way to understand more fully the processes within an officer's 'habitus'. Sackmann (1991) presents culture as the collection of shared organizational knowledge, the 'collective construction of social reality' (cited in Chan 1997: 76). While this cultural knowledge is located in the habitus of an individual, it is constructed through the interactions of the organizational group. This has four dimensions: dictionary knowledge, directory knowledge, recipe knowledge, and axiomatic knowledge. 'Dictionary knowledge' for the police refers to how they categorize and label people and events which they encounter. This can emerge as stereotyping while the police attempt to make complex situations and problems more manageable. 'Directory knowledge' utilizes dictionary knowledge in order to determine what is and is not appropriate behaviour in others and then serves as a guide as to what is the usual action for an officer to take in that situation. It is a type of instruction manual for how operational work is normally carried out. 'Recipe knowledge' has a normative dimension, and it indicates to an officer what should or should not be done in particular circumstances and suggests ways of coping with police work. One example is the police 'code of silence' which protects a fellow officer who has been accused of misconduct. 'Axiomatic knowledge' refers to the 'police mandate', the fundamental purpose of the policing organization. This can include the sense that they are there to wage 'a war' on crime and to protect the vulnerable. Often held by senior managers, axiomatic knowledge provides the foundation for the organization and shapes its goals (Chan 1997).

Chan (1997), like Bourdieu, sees the habitus a relational concept. The cultural knowledge described above does not exist in static form, but is shaped and revised in light of the officer's own experiences (including through police practice) and changes in the policing field. Bourdieu (Bourdieu and Wacquant 1992) describes the field as a social space where actors compete for power or influence. For the police, it will include historical social relationships with communities (e.g. between the police organization and minority groups), changes to legislation that affects police work (e.g. cannabis being downgraded in terms of its importance as a controlled substance), or reform of police governing structures (e.g. the introduction of Police and Crime Commissioners in England and Wales in 2012). Some aspects of the field, such as legislation or governance structures, are objective factors which serve as anchors to the social relationships in question. Changes in the field will have an influence on habitus, but likewise, changes in the habitus of police officers can have an impact on the field. Chan (1997) proposes that both of these influence and can be influenced by police practice, and so all three exist in a dynamic relationship, with the police officer at the core (Chan 1997).

Field, Habitus, and Practice for Police Community Support Officers

Chan's theoretical framework as described above is a useful tool through which to integrate the discussions from Chapter 4 on institutional undermining with that from Chapter 5 on complementary and competitive teams. The process of institutional undermining which the PCSOs experience is an aspect of the field. Decisions at the organizational level, such as how much training PCSOs should have, what powers they will be allowed, and their management structures, are objective and historical elements of a police force which will shape PCSOs' experiences (Chan 1997).

While PCSOs may be able to exercise some degree of influence on these, they largely represent forces at a macro-level for which the net effect was to undermine the PCSO role from the beginning.

The PCSO response to this particular configuration of the field was discussed in Chapter 5. PCSOs in the various neighbourhood policing teams (NPTs) work in separate performance teams (Goffman 1959) from their police officer counterparts. However, the nature of the relationships between the PCSO and the PC teams varied, with some being more complementary (mutually supportive and social) and some being more competitive (not sharing resources and often hoarding information). These configurations of competitive or complementary teams reflect the habitus of those PCSOs. For example, in NPTs with complementary teams, PCSOs' recipe knowledge (Sackmann 1991) will suggest that they should share information that they have collected about potential offenders in the local area directly with the community police officers. In NPTs with a competitive configuration, however, recipe knowledge will suggest that this information should be withheld from direct communication with PCs and instead only be registered on the intelligence database. Therefore, the policing field includes elements at the NPT level which will interact with and influence the construction of the habitus of the PCSOs working there. This will result in particular practices for the police officers and PCSOs. These practices will in turn influence the PCSOs' habitus and the field of policing for that NPT.

A further example of the degree to which the field is influenced by elements at the NPT level is through the role of supervisors. Managers, such as sergeants and inspectors, are a part of the field of policing (Chan 1997), and they can have an important role in shaping the experiences of the police officers and PCSOs in their team (van Hulst 2017), which will then contribute to the development of the habitus, as well as to their practice. Managers can create workplace environments which bring the separate performance teams closer together, for example, by insisting that all officers and staff share the same open-plan office or by encouraging PCs to undertake joint patrols with PCSOs. These arrangements can encourage the performance teams to operate in a complementary way. Managers can also exacerbate difficult relationships between the PC and PCSO teams by, for example, taking the word of a PC over that of a PCSO in a dispute or appearing to monitor the movements of PCSOs more closely than that of the PCs in the NPT. This will encourage competitive relationships between the teams. PCSOs' direct experiences of their managers will also shape their habitus such as through the level of access they have to patrol cars, the time they are allowed for meal breaks, and to which beat areas they are assigned. These are aspects of the policing field which have local, NPT level variations and will thus influence how PCSOs develop their habitus and their practice within that policing team. The reactions of PCSOs to these management decisions, in turn, will have a degree of influence on the field. It should be noted of course that while management officers shape the field of policing for other officers and staff, as police officers themselves, they, too, are shaped by the field in terms of their own habitus and practice. Their positons as managers can give them a more significant degree of influence in the field, however, than that enjoyed by PCSOs or officers lower in the institutional hierarchy.

Occupational Culture as Meaning Construction

While Chan's (1997) framework is useful for integrating institutional undermining and complementary/competitive teams, it misses an important element of occupational culture: the actual process of how field and habitus are reconciled within an individual and how this is brought to bear on policing practice. Language and discursive interaction are central to this process (Maitlis and Christianson 2014), as noted by Shearing and Ericson (1991) in relation to the importance of storytelling in occupational culture. Chan (1997, 2003) mentions the work of Shearing and Ericson in her text, as demonstrating how police officers are active agents in the construction of their culture, but their work does not form a central part of her framework. Stories bring meaning to events and difficult experiences, and as Maitlis and Christianson (2014) indicate, this is important to consider because in doing so we are:

> uncovering the very different stories told by different groups and showing how even a dominant organizational narrative can be embellished and modified by less powerful individuals in ways that significantly change its meaning. (81)

As earlier discussions in this book have demonstrated, storytelling is a regular feature of police organizations. Both police officers and

PCSOs engage in stories to process and give meaning to their work and their experiences, and to pass on lessons to other members of their performance team (Goffman 1959; van Hulst 2013, 2017). This was the case, for example, in Chapter 5, when PCSO Alfie was talking about his experiences of PCSO Trudy, who, in his words, 'has one day on and 12 days off', thus making clear to the others that the role requires an expected level of dedication.

This process of meaning construction through stories which then leads to relevant actions reflects the dynamic model Chan (1997, 2003) developed, but it adds an important additional element to it. In Chan's framework, changes in the policing field influence the habitus of officers (and staff) who then enact those changes (or not) in their policing practice. These changes can then bring a degree of influence back to the field, in that the role of the officers and staff within in it may have altered. Chan (2007) later proposes that a theory of sensemaking could be used to better understand the relationship between the field and the habitus in respect of the actual process of reconciling changes in the field with the structure of the habitus. Sensemaking is indeed a useful concept, but it tends to emphasize how occupational groups cope with change. I would argue that stories and storytelling are more useful in understanding the ongoing and constant task of reconciliation between field and habitus experienced by PCSOs in their daily effort to perform their usefulness to others. Examining Chan's original model (1997) through the storytelling lens, we see that it is the 'process' of meaning construction and the 'development' of actions in response to that meaning where occupational culture is located. The responses to this process are products or artefacts (in Schein's (1990) terms) of that culture, rather than being culture themselves. Culture is an active and creative process undertaken by individuals or groups in the course of discursive interactions. So in Chan's model, Sackmann's (1991) conception of 'cultural knowledge' is useful in terms of what emerges from the process of meaning construction and how it develops the habitus, but is not in itself police organizational culture. Culture is the process that was undertaken to develop the cultural knowledge which then guides future actions in the field and in practice. A fuller consideration of storytelling reveals this process for both PCSOs and police officers.

Occupational Culture in Pluralized Policing

PCSOs have demonstrated a variety of cultural responses to their occupational experiences, whether these represent macro- or micro-level activity. These responses are unique to them as members of police staff, and they reflect the complementary or competitive nature of their performance teams (as discussed in Chapter 5). The case of identity threat to PCSOs will provide a useful example. The PCSOs who participated in this research, in the main, expressed a sense of shock upon joining the police organization at the way they were treated either in training or when they were assigned to their beat areas (Chapter 4). They were not valued as members of the policing 'family' as they had thought they would be or afforded the levels of support that they saw being offered to PCs.

For PCSOs who are based in the more complementary performance teams, such as that in Starrybridge, the way they attempt to reconcile the misalignment between their expectations of their occupational identity and the reality (as the organization sees it) is to engage in dramatic realization (Goffman 1959). As mentioned in Chapter 5, this is where members of a performance team will highlight the more exciting and engaging aspects of their role through stories in order to enhance their identity claims. For PCSOs, this will include examples of law enforcement activity such as tracking suspected burglars, extensive evidence gathering, or assistance with arrests (see also Cosgrove and Ramshaw 2013). They will often work with PCs in the course of these activities. These actions and the resulting stories reflect a sense within the PCSOs that they must prove their worth to their police officer colleagues as the organization cannot be assumed to accept their identity claims as the PCSOs would wish it to. These PCSOs are attempting to reduce the gap between their identity expectations and reality by changing the nature of the reality. They are willing to do this and will invest a great deal of time and energy in these dramatic moments, which are then revealed to colleagues back in the station. These stories are also employed for PCSOs to convince themselves that their initial identity expectations are still true. Police officers also engage in dramatic storytelling (Shearing and Ericson 1991; van Hulst 2013), but the reasons for this are different to that of PCSOs. Police officers will engage in stories to make sense of their role and their experiences, whereas PCSOs do it (in this case) to justify their existence.

The actions taken by PCSOs in competitive performance teams to address the misalignment between their organizational identity and the reality of their situation are different. These PCSOs have not only experienced a threat to their identity upon joining the service, this is then exacerbated when they are placed in NPTs with police officers who are not willing to engage with them as equal partners in policing work or with supervisors who do not seem to support them. For example, I was told a story by PCSO Paul (in Marshton) about how a PC accused the PCSOs of using a flat given to them for meetings by a local housing estate landlord for taking extended breaks and thus to avoid work. PCSO Paul said their supervisor took the word of the PC without asking the PCSOs for their explanation (field note 21/11). PCSOs in teams such as these, as was the case in Marshton and Fayhaven, tended to exercise their PCSO tasks so as to meet basic expectations of their supervisors, but would avoid engaging in work that went beyond this. For example, they would not contemplate interrupting a meal break to attend a call from the dispatch operator, they do not work past their scheduled shift time, and they avoid confrontations with members of the public as much as possible as they cannot assume that the organization will support them (e.g. by responding to a call for assistance quickly or backing them up if there is a complaint later). In this case, stories are used to justify the resulting actions rather than to dramatize their work (van Hulst 2013). Although the 'work to rule' approach (a cultural artefact) has been identified in police officers in typology studies (such as that of Muir (1977), who describes the 'Avoider' officer in this way) this approach by PCSOs again reflects a different motivation. Police officers do not need to reconcile their existence in the way that PCSOs do. For PCSOs, their basic occupational identity has been questioned to such a degree, as revealed by stories such as the one above, that they do not see any reason to try to change the views of their police colleagues. They thus reduce the gap between expectations and reality by lowering their own expectations of their occupational identity.

The case of threatened occupational identity (Maitlis and Christianson 2014) shows that while the outcomes, or artefacts, of occupational culture may at times be similar for PCs and PCSOs (e.g. employing dramatic realization or work to rule orientations), the process of meaning construction which leads to these outcomes is different for these groups. It is this process of attributing meaning to workplace experiences where culture is located. Thus while there are many similarities in the field and habitus for PCs and PCSOs (see e.g. Cosgrove's (2015) work on PCSO typologies and their similarities to those of PCs), their respective occupational cultures are different.

This does not mean, however, that the artefacts of occupational culture for PCSOs and PCs are always the same. There are some interesting differences which emerged from this research. As has been discussed previously, not only were newly recruited PCSOs faced with an organization that did not support them in the way that they expected, many also discovered that the role itself was ill-defined. There is also a significant degree of variability in how the role is performed nationally, as each chief constable has a degree of discretion in the range of powers allocated to the PCSOs in his or her police force.[1] Chapter 3 describes what PCSOs do, and for many this involved creating a role for themselves to cope with this ambiguity. These PCSOs developed a niche in their beats, for example, as negotiators in neighbour disputes, or by developing an awareness of local vulnerable adults on whom they would check at regular intervals. Some would actively build a group of trusted informants (Key Informant Networks) in the area or make a point of monitoring particularly problematic families. PCs are not faced with this same degree of ambiguity in their role, both locally and nationally, and so do not need to look for a focus in their work. The PCSOs who wanted to be busy in their beats would find a way to do so.[2] This resulted in some creative ways to serve their local communities which may not be replicated by other PCSOs in their area.

An additional difference in the cultural artefacts of the PCSOs and PCs relates to their conceptions of space and time. PCSOs are meant primarily to be a visible presence in their beat areas, and the main method by which they achieve this is through visible foot patrol. There are restrictions on how often and in what

[1] This situation has deepened with the Policing and Crime Act 2017, to be discussed further in Chapter 7.

[2] This need to find things to do when faced with a lack of direction is no longer a prominent issue since the 2010 funding cuts and subsequent staff reductions. The current situation for PCSOs will be discussed in more detail in Chapter 7.

circumstance PCSOs can use police cars, and so their main method of transportation is usually bus, bicycle, or on foot. PCs do not face these same restrictions (or at least not to the same degree) and so can find themselves travelling great distances during the course of a shift, or spending long periods of time in cars. PCSOs, on the other hand, need to be aware of how far they need to travel to do their daily work and how long it will take to get there. This means (as was discussed in Chapter 5) that they must carefully plan ahead in terms of where they can take their meal breaks, as they may need to take their meal with them when they leave the police station at the start of a shift. PCSOs in rural areas had more access to police cars, but this was not guaranteed at all times. All PCSOs tended to develop a network of toilet stops in their areas—places where they knew they would be allowed to use the facilities without question, or places where they would be welcome to take their breaks. Police constables also will do this (Cain 1973), but it is not quite as crucial for their daily comfort as it is for PCSOs. In addition, the PCSO craft is highly dependent on knowledge of the local area, both in terms of the residents there and in relation to how the beat is structured in space and the movement of people within that space. It is through building knowledge of people and spaces that PCSOs can prove their worth to police constables, should they subsequently become aware of criminal activity or receive useful information about crimes in their beats. Geography is thus both a challenge and an opportunity for PCSOs.

Conceptions of space and time as cultural artefacts can also vary between PCs and PCSOs at the more abstract level. Chapter 5 explored the backstage regions which are used and created by the PCSO and PC interaction teams within police stations. PCSOs in NPTs with complementary teams freely shared internal police spaces with the PCs, but in the more competitive arrangements, PCSOs carefully protected their spaces. This could be seen in the small 'PCSO only' office in Marshton, or in the way PCs would avoid the breakroom in Fayhaven when the PCSOs were using it. These PCSOs tended to plan the timing of their breaks in advance so that they could all be in the room together. Time was another aspect where differences with PCs could be noted at an abstract level. PCSO Tim in Fallhill described to me how PCSOs were keenly aware that any interaction that they have in a community could leave a legacy (field note 20/10). These members of staff patrol and work in the same areas for long periods (over the course of years in some cases) and so need to find a careful balance between enforcement activity and community building so as not to unnecessarily damage relationships with communities. Theirs is the long view. PCs, on the other hand, were more likely to enter and leave beat areas quickly and were less sensitive to what the long-term repercussions of their actions might be for those areas. This was especially the case for response officers (although it is less so for PCs involved in partnership work, see O'Neill and McCarthy (2014)) or community police officers in competitive team arrangements. Thus their awareness of time was more immediate.

A final difference which I will explore in the expressions of PCSO culture compared to that of PCs (although there are others) relates to how they view their commitment to their jobs. Previous police culture writers (e.g. Manning 1977; Reiner 2010; Loftus 2009) describe the police 'sense of mission' whereby being a police officer is less a job and more a calling or a moral crusade (see also Crank 2004; Brogden et al 1988). Police officers can see themselves as the only barrier between the weak and vulnerable and those who would seek to prey on them. PCSOs, in contrast, many of whom were very dedicated to their work, tended to describe it as primarily 'a job'. Several of the participants in this research had held employment in other fields prior to becoming PCSOs, in some cases for decades. Other PCSOs were younger and viewed the PCSO role as a step towards a more interesting and demanding job later, such as becoming a police officer. Very few of the participants seemed to view their PCSO work as a calling that registered with them on a personal level, no matter how committed they were to their communities. It thus lacked the same sense of mission that has been detected in the cultural expressions of police officers. This reflects a process of meaning construction for PCSOs who, unlike police officers, find themselves in an organization which presents them as the less valuable members and, more recently, as expendable.

Conclusion

This discussion of PCSO occupational culture is not exhaustive, but is intended to give an indication of the process through which it is formed and can be expressed by these members of staff within pluralized public policing fields. PCSOs, like PCs, will engage in processes of meaning construction through storytelling in the course of their work in policing. These processes are different for PCSOs, and the resulting actions and cultural artefacts (Sackmann's (1991) 'cultural knowledge') may at times be similar to that of police officers or may differ. However, as PCSOs have experienced a different route to reconciling their habitus with the policing field (Chan 1997), these staff members will have a different occupational culture, as found through storytelling, than that of police officers. As we have explored here, how exactly the outcomes of their meaning construction are expressed will further depend on whether the PCSOs are part of complementary or competitive performance teams in their NPTs, and it will be shaped by decisions of supervisors, who occupy a role in the policing field.

By adding emphasis to the processes of storytelling (Shearing and Ericson 1991; van Hulst 2013) to Chan's (1997) model for constructing police culture, a more complete account can be made for the different, albeit at times similar, cultural expressions from the various members of the pluralized field of public policing. This field will comprise elements from the national and more local scales, and the actors engaging with it include police officers, PCSOs, Special Constables, and other members of police staff and affiliated roles (Crawford et al 2005; Crawford 2008; Rogers 2017). These actors will change, and have changed over time, as will the type of work that they do and the nature of the wider policing field itself. It is thus important that any analysis of policing cultures takes into account new developments, especially on the national scale. It is to a consideration of the current state of community policing that we now turn, as well as to a look at the implications of this analysis for police studies more broadly in this and other countries.

7

The Culture of Contemporary Community and Plural Policing

The research explored in this book was conducted in 2012–2013, at a time when significant changes in public policing in England and Wales were starting to unfold. It is important to consider what has happened in the intervening years and how the analysis presented in this text applies to this new context. However, the findings of this research have implications beyond the UK, which will also be examined. Community policing specifically and pluralized policing more broadly are topics that have expression in a number of countries and contexts. It is important to recognize that while they are indeed separate arenas of research and practice, community policing is itself a pluralized method of policing in relation to its variability internationally and because it involves multiple actors (both in terms of the police and in terms of their partner agencies). There is thus an unavoidable degree of overlap between the two concepts. This final chapter will therefore consider what this study of Police Community Support Officers (PCSOs) can offer for current scholarship and discourse on both community and pluralized policing beyond the UK, and the necessity of considering occupational culture within these, using the framework developed in the previous chapters.

What Is Community Policing Now?

Before considering the wider implications of this research on PCSOs for conceptions of community and plural policing in the UK and elsewhere, it is important to recognize the challenges and changes which occurred after the fieldwork for this book took place. Two of the most significant changes were the introduction of Police and Crime Commissioners (PCCs) in 2012 to replace Police Authorities, and the lifting of the budget ring-fence for neighbourhood policing, which accompanied the arrival of PCCs (Higgins 2017). The PCC role was introduced in England and Wales just before this project started, and PCCs took up office in early 2013, just as the fieldwork for this project was ending. PCCs are elected by the residents of a police force area to hold the chief constable to account (in contrast to Police Authorities, which were appointed) and to make decisions on budget allocation for the force. This meant that the central direction from the UK government as to how policing should be funded was dropped to allow for local focus and variations. The intention was to make policing more accountable to and reflective of the local areas. It also meant that there was no longer a national vision for neighbourhood policing, and considerable further variation began to appear in how it was structured (Higgins 2017, 2018).

In addition to the changes to policing governance discussed above, policing in England and Wales in general, and neighbourhood policing in particular, have experienced significant reductions in staff and resources since the 2010 budget review (O'Neill 2014b; Greig-Midlane 2014). Between 2010 and 2015, central government funding for policing reduced overall by 20%. A wide range of adjustments was made to cope with this reduced resource, some of which involved reductions or reallocation of staff as well as recruitment freezes (HMIC 2014; Higgins 2018). Police officers cannot be made redundant, so those who left policing for other reasons (retirement, dismissal, or resignation) were usually not replaced. PCSOs, in contrast, as members of civilian staff, can be subject to redundancy. Most police forces in England and Wales took this route (to varying degrees) to reduce overall salary expenses. The combination of reduced numbers of PCSOs and police officers, as well as police officers being tasked with a wider range of roles and responsibilities (to cover for the loss of colleagues, as well as support staff), has had a dramatic effect on the nature, composition, and work of neighbourhood policing teams (NPTs) (Higgins 2017 and 2018).

Table 1 below indicates the change in police officer and PCSO numbers from their height in 2010 to the most recent figures in 2017.

As the table indicates, there has been on average a 40% reduction in the number of PCSOs in England and Wales from 2010 to 2017. At the same time, there has been a 14% reduction in the total number of police officers. The exact level of staff loss per police force will vary within this, of course (Higgins 2017). For example, North Yorkshire Police had 198 PCSOs in 2010 and 181

Table 1 Police Officer and Police Community Support Officer Numbers (Full-Time Equivalents) in England and Wales from 31 March 2010 to 31 March 2017

Date	Police officers	PCSOs
	N (FTE)	N (FTE)
31-Mar-10	143,734	16,918
31-Mar-11	139,110	15,820
31-Mar-12	134,100	14,393
31-Mar-13	129,584	14,205
31-Mar-14	127,909	13,066
31-Mar-15	127,192	12,370
31-Mar-16	124,066	11,043
31-Mar-17	123,142	10,213

Abbreviation: FTE, full-time equivalents.

Source: Police Workforce England and Wales Statistics (The Home Office, multiple dates): https://www.gov.uk/government/collections/police-workforce-england-and-wales.

in 2017, a reduction of 8.5%. In contrast, the Metropolitan Police in London had 4,645 PCSOs in 2010 and only 1,442 in 2017, a reduction of 69% (Home Office 2010, 2017). Regardless, this scale of police officer and staff reductions, particularly in relation to PCSOs, has led to significant changes to policing practice, as police forces tended to move resources with a view to protecting 'frontline' policing services. This has meant a focus on reactive crime-control methods over preventative and partnership-oriented approaches (HMIC 2014).

As was discussed in Chapter 1, neighbourhood policing in England and Wales was designed so that every geographical division in every police force had allocated NPTs with dedicated community police officers, supervisors (sergeants and inspectors), PCSOs, Special Constables, and, in some cases, office support staff. These officers and staff were not to be seconded to other work unless necessary. While neighbourhood policing (and community policing in the USA) has not shown a direct effect on the crime rate, it has been shown to improve police and community relationships (if it is done well, see Foster and Jones (2010)). While neighbourhood policing did not follow exactly the same format in every force in England and Wales (Higgins 2017), visible foot patrol was often a main element. Other aspects included problem-oriented policing and collaboration with public sector and other partners (Longstaff et al 2015; Mason 2009; see College of Policing 2018 for guidelines on neighbourhood policing). It is with these preventative and 'slow burn' methods with which PCSOs did most of their work, as they are not able to investigate crime, use force, or make arrests. Therefore, when nearly every police force in England and Wales reduces their preventative and community-oriented work, the remit of PCSOs, which, in effect, is declared disposable. An extreme example of this is Norfolk Constabulary, which, from 31 March 2018, eliminated the PCSO role.[1] To date this is the only police force to take this option.

For those PCSOs who remain in police forces, there has been a further blurring of their powers, roles, and responsibilities in recent months than was the case previously. As Chapter 1 mentioned, PCSOs in all police forces in England and Wales were conferred initially with a specific range of powers, but there was an additional 'optional' range of powers which could be granted at the wish of the local chief constable. This meant that there was a degree of variation between police forces, as some PCSOs had every power possible, whereas others could be quite limited (and many configurations in between). For example, the ability to detain a person for up to 30 minutes while waiting for a police constable to arrive was one of the 'optional' powers that not all police forces adopted. Since the 2010 budget reform and the subsequent reductions of police officers and PCSOs, the PCSOs which remain find that they are taking on roles and responsibilities which had previously been within the remit of the neighbourhood police officers. This could include, for example, conducting investigations in cases of low-level crime (Higgins 2018). In many places, NPTs were effectively disbanded, and police constables now have both community and response

[1] https://www.norfolk.police.uk/news/latest-news/29-03-2018/police-chief-pays-tribute-pcsos-2020-plans-take-effect.

roles.[2] PCSOs are left to cover the work of the neighbourhood officers (although not that which requires arrest or other PC-only tasks), meaning that they have less time to be self-directed or go on extended visible patrol, making their community engagement work more difficult to sustain. It also means that the lines between PCSO and PC are blurring further, but again with great variability nationally depending on the extent of local staff reductions (Higgins 2018).

Recent legislation has compounded this situation, however. The Policing and Crime Act (2017) has inverted the method by which it is decided what differentiates a PCSO from a PC. Instead of listing which powers a PCSO has (or can have), this legislation stipulates which powers are the exclusive reserve of police constables. Any other power previously conferred to police officers or PCSOs can now be granted to PCSOs, subject to the wishes of the chief constable in question. This includes the use of CS and PAVA spray. It is yet unclear the extent to which PCSO powers will be expanded in light of the legislation. In addition, new powers also require new training to support their implementation, which has a cost implication. Therefore, it may be the case that there is not a rush to adopt more powers for PCSOs, but it will only take a few police forces to do so to further confuse what it means to be a PCSO for the public, police officers, and the PCSOs themselves. For example, Dorset Police have introduced the role of 'Police Community Support Investigators'. These are PCSOs who have been given additional training to undertake a range of criminal investigation tasks and to speak to victims of crime at predetermined appointments.[3] They thus represent a formal development of the PCSO role that takes them closer to being like a police officer by adopting some of the powers which had previously been unavailable to PCSOs.

It has been argued that the loss of clearly defined neighbourhood policing practice supported by PCSOs is, or can be, detrimental to policing in general (Higgins 2018; Colover and

[2] See Higgins (2017, 2018) for a full typological analysis of neighbourhood policing configurations.

[3] https://www.policeoracle.com/news/local_and_neighbourhood_policing/2018/Apr/19/Force-introduces-new-Police-Community-Support-Investigator-role_97557.html.html.

Quinton 2018). Neighbourhood policing and PCSOs endeavour to build connections in communities which can develop trust between the two and potentially lead to information (intelligence) sharing in some cases (O'Neill 2014b; Greig-Midlane 2014; HMIC 2014; Longstaff et al 2015). Both the erosion of neighbourhood policing as a distinct method and the reduction of PCSOs could significantly inhibit these community engagement methods and the long-term benefits they can generate. Millie (2013), in contrast, has argued that it is not necessarily the case that policing will be harmed by resource reductions. As he points out, police numbers grew by a third over the last four decades, even though the general population only grew by 10% during that time. In addition, the overall remit of the police has expanded significantly, especially since the mid-1990s. Millie (2013) suggests that this may be the time to consider narrowing the police remit to those tasks which only the police can do, and to restrict other work (the more 'social service' side of the job) to the agencies, community groups, or volunteers which are better placed to address them. Millie (2013) gives the examples of probation work, work with schools, and event security which have been included in the policing 'mission creep', or 'policification' of social policy, since the New Labour government was in power. While such an argument is logical, the reality of police work means that it is not simple to differentiate between 'real' police work and everything else the police do. In addition, the police are available to the public 24 hours a day, and it is unrealistic to expect other services to provide this kind of cover for the social problems which arise outside of standard working hours. Millie (2013) notes that funding would have to be moved from policing to other services in order to achieve the proposed narrowing. However, as all public services were affected by the 2010 budget reductions, it is unlikely that they would have the capacity to pick up more work and expand hours, even with some additional resources. A better method might be to find ways to achieve deeper integration of the public sector services so that partnership and co-production are a more regular and ongoing occurrence, and scarce resources are shared more effectively. PCSOs in particular are well-placed to do this kind of work, and this further points to the need to support and develop these staff (as was argued in Chapter 4).

The Cultural Implications of the Further Pluralization of Public Policing

The pluralization of public policing in England and Wales is continuing in both the types of actors involved in public policing, as well as in relation to the role and powers available to each. The Policing and Crime Act (2017) has not only broadened the rage of powers open to PCSOs (discussed above), it has also introduced the roles of 'community support volunteer', 'policing support officer', and 'policing support volunteer'. The community support volunteer is in effect a PCSO who volunteers to do the role rather than be paid for it. They have the same range of powers as paid PCSOs. Policing support officers and policing support volunteers represent an amalgamation of the previous investigating officer, detention officer, and escort officer (support staff) roles. The range of powers open to these staff is more limited than that for PCSOs, but now there is also the potential for volunteers to do the same range of tasks as the paid staff. The increase in volunteer positions in policing is one way for police forces to attempt to meet public expectations for policing services but within the context of constrained budgets.

The key issue here is that for the first time, policing volunteers, beyond Special Constables, have the same range of powers as the paid staff they reflect. This had not been the case previously, which meant that PCSO and other policing support staff tasks were the preserve of paid employees. The Policing and Crime Act (2017) has now changed this landscape. The 'policing family' has been further diversified, and there are more (or there could be more) unpaid members of this occupational family. As with the debates which have been present for Special Constables for decades (Gill and Mawby 1990; Bullock and Leeney 2014), the ability of volunteers to do the same work and have the same powers as paid PCSO staff can be seen to call into question whether the role is as valued and as central to community policing as it is intended to be. Moreover, it potentially threatens the terms and conditions for the paid staff.

At the time of writing, the community support volunteer role is too new to have been evaluated to assess its impact in community policing or its effect on the work and working conditions of paid PCSOs. However, Lincolnshire Police ran a trial and an evaluation of what was then called the Volunteer Police Community Support Officer. These volunteers did similar work to PCSOs and had PCSO mentors during their training. However, as the role was developed prior to the change in legislation, they did not have the powers PCSOs do, and this was regarded as inhibiting their potential value (Strudwick et al 2017). The evaluation of the VPCSO project also identified the potential friction which could occur if volunteers were able to do the same work (with powers) as paid PCSOs do, because of the threat this might pose to the long-term viability of the paid PCSO role (Strudwick et al 2017). A further consideration is whether volunteers will be able to develop the same connections to and knowledge of local communities in the way that full-time paid PCSOs do, as this is regarded as one of the core elements of the job. Volunteers tend to work only a few hours a week, as they may have full-time jobs or other commitments elsewhere. This lack of regular presence in beat areas could undermine the time-intensive trust-building and engagement work that is intended to be one of the advantages of the PCSO role over that of police constables.

The combination of an overall erosion of neighbourhood policing since 2010 (Higgins 2018), a 40% reduction in PCSO numbers, greater national variability in the role and powers for PCSOs, and the arrival of community support volunteers has led to a situation where the 'institutional undermining' of PCSOs (as discussed in Chapter 4) has been 'enhanced' since the research for this book was conducted. While some police forces have made a concerted effort to retain neighbourhood policing structures as much as possible, in most police forces, preventative and problem-oriented policing has been de-emphasized in favour of enforcement-oriented work (Higgins 2018). As Cosgrave and Ramshaw (2013) point out, an emphasis on enforcement activity undermines PCSOs, as their official role and the policy around them does not allow for this. Therefore, the type of police work for which PCSOs are ideally suited is rapidly diminishing, meaning that the need to justify their own existence is further heightened for PCSOs. This will have a direct effect on their relationships with police officers. PCSOs in 'competitive teams' (discussed in Chapter 5) are likely to have even fewer resources and support for their work while also being tasked with more to do (to supplement the drop in police officer numbers). Their 'work to rule' cultural response (discussed in Chapter 6) is likely to be further ingrained in this situation as their work-place experiences are likely to be more, rather than less, stressful. PCSOs in 'complementary teams' might find it more difficult to sustain their integrated position with PCs, owing to similar pressures on resources and an overall loss of PCs. Many may also now be located in larger police stations (because of station closures) and so could have lost their close connections to the police officer colleagues they had in the small local stations. This will inhibit their opportunities for 'dramatic realization'. While they may still have the highly valued dramatic enforcement-style situations that they can tell stories about, they may not be as socially integrated with PCs as they used to be. This could mean fewer opportunities for telling their stories and a more difficult audience to convince about their performances when they do. PCSOs in these teams may be losing their status as complementing the work of community officers and instead find themselves supplementing it. This could result in fewer complementary interaction teams in plural public policing overall and a greater number of competitive ones. Further ethnographic work is needed to ascertain the exact effects of the recent funding, governance, and legislative changes on the cultural responses of PCSOs. However, the picture so far is one where there is now an enhanced plurality of roles involved in public policing (with the arrival of community support volunteers) and an enhanced plurality of the powers and remit of PCSOs nationally. This is likely to be a more stressful working situation for PCSOs that will have significant implications for their occupational cultural responses, which includes their relationships with police officers and includes how they undertake their policing practice.

Conclusion: Implications for International Policing Practice

The primary objects of study for this book have been PCSOs, neighbourhood policing, and the pluralization of public policing in England and Wales. However, as community policing, specifically, and pluralized policing, more generally, are phenomena encountered in other policing fields across the globe, there are broader lessons to be gained from this work. Each of these will be considered in turn, including a consideration of the role occupational culture can play in the success (or not) of these.

Community policing is a method which is being identified as 'good practice' in a number of countries (see e.g. Brodgen and Nijhar 2005; Bayerl et al 2017). Identifying 'core' components of community policing can be difficult, as it tends to vary considerably from one context to another (O'Neill 2010; but see College of Policing 2018, for recent guidelines). This is of course to be expected as each 'community' in question will likewise vary, as will standard policing practice for that region (community policing is thus itself pluralized). However, the primary purpose of community policing is to focus on preventative approaches which engage publics as much as possible (policing 'with' and 'for' rather than 'on' or 'to'). This type of work tends to be slower and more focused on longer-term outcomes, rather than fast, reactive, and oriented around short-term (or immediate) problems. This study of PCSOs and their role in the neighbourhood policing project demonstrates what can be gained if this method of policing is done well and with dedicated resources. While not all public policing jurisdictions will be able to have a proportion of police officers or auxiliary staff who are engaged in community policing to the complete exclusion of reactive methods, a degree of dedicated resources means that the officers (and in some places, staff) who do community policing are well-placed to fulfil the method to its potential.

Working with partner organizations and communities to solve local problems, often an aspect of community policing, takes time, and success is difficult to measure. For example, there are no arrest rates or crimes that have been 'solved' which can be measured quantitatively. It is more likely that outcomes are community members who feel safer or young people who feel more included in their communities (Innes 2005). Officers and staff engaged in community work need the appropriate facilities, opportunities, and skill set, and they cannot be held to the same outcome measurements as reactive officers and staff. To try to meld reactive policing with long-term preventative policing is difficult to do without detriment to the long-term method. However, this 'slow burn' policing approach can yield the outcomes needed to reduce public demand in the first place, for example, through gathering information on local crimes from communities with whom the police have built relationships of trust, and through collaborative work with public sector or other partners (O'Neill 2014b). Not all police officers or staff members have the ideal skill set for this work, so those assigned to it either need dedicated training or need to be selected carefully (O'Neill and McCarthy 2014). While this text did not assess the effectiveness of community policing, it did reveal what can be achieved by officers and staff who are committed to and well-resourced to undertake it. It has also revealed how community policing can be inhibited when the needed organizational and social support is missing.

The lessons from this book extend beyond operational practice, however. Chapter 1 explored the existing scholarship on plural policing. These debates have included the rise and significance of the private policing sector, the governance of policing (both public and private), and the development of new roles in public policing. What has largely been missing from these discussions is the occupational cultural landscape within these for all of the groups in question. This book has argued that this culture and the resulting expressions of it are created through the interplay of macro and micro factors for the groups in question, which are processed and reconciled through storytelling. By building on the work of Goffman (1959), Chan (1997), and the literature on storytelling (e.g. that of Shearing and Ericson 1991; van Hulst 2013), a framework has been developed (in Chapters 4–6) to structure and analyse occupational cultures within pluralized policing (e.g. that undertaken in community policing). Goffman's dramaturgic metaphor is used to present the interaction patterns of the policing groups and to illustrate exactly how they operate as separate performance teams (in the case of PCSOs and PCs, these performance teams could be complementary or competitive). These interaction patterns form part of each group's 'habitus', as described by Chan, while the macro factors (including choices made by the organization broadly and management more locally) form part of the interaction 'field'. By examining the role of 'storytelling', we can better understand the processes by which culture is created through the reconciling of the field and habitus. This process of meaning construction will be different for each policing group and will further vary by local context. In the research here, for example, PCSOs were primarily motivated by a need to justify their existence, which was not the case for PCs, because of their unique experiences of 'institutional undermining'. The expressions of the various occupational cultures, the cultural artefacts, may be similar at times (e.g. when both PCs and PCSOs show a preference for enforcement activity), but there are also important differences. This framework will advance understanding of how occupational culture in the context of similar, but separate, groups involved in pluralized policing is created, sustained, or modified over time and in specific locations.

The findings from this research study further indicate that a careful analysis of how the various members of the 'extended policing family' build an occupational culture and interact with each other is crucial in order to understand fully how pluralized policing is structured, and the effect of this on practice. This will not just apply to the variety of roles within public policing (e.g. PCSOs, police constables and volunteers); it also includes police relationships with partners and with members of the private sector. For example, the extent to which these groups are integrated and collaborate in supportive ways will have implications for how well they achieve mutually beneficial outcomes in their work. Crucially, the nature of these relationships is not predetermined and can be influenced by managerial and institutional choices. Moving towards operational and institutional contexts which support complementary (rather than competitive) working methods is to be encouraged because performance teams within pluralized public policing which collaborate well and support each other tend to have better outcomes in terms of staff morale and a freer sharing of information and resources.

As we have seen in the observational research reported here, if PCSOs feel supported in their work, they are more likely to take an active interest in it, look for areas of creativity in their interactions with the community, and actively gather and pass on highly valued 'intelligence', thus potentially enhancing the service the public receives, as well as furthering crime-control priorities. Staff members who feel isolated from other policing groups and who feel unsupported by their organization generally are not as inclined to work collaboratively with colleagues and will become quickly disillusioned with the job itself as they will not have the time or resources necessary to fully embrace their role. This points to the importance of a fuller and deeper understanding of the role of occupational culture in shaping how policing policy and organizational structures are interpreted by the various actors involved in pluralized policing arenas and expressed in their practice. This argument has been made in relation to police officers for some time (see e.g. O'Neill et al 2007), but it is also clearly, if not more, relevant in the case of multiple policing roles operating in a pluralized public policing context. Community policing is one example of pluralized policing, but it is not the only one.

The analysis here will thus apply beyond community policing to areas of work such as transport policing or the policing of mass private property (Wakefield 2003), among others. How each group member in a particular context is initiated, trained, integrated (both internally and externally), and developed will shape occupational culture and thus the resulting cultural expressions of that culture. These cultural expressions can influence the extent to which a particular policing policy, initiative, or organization achieves its desired aims. Failure to examine meaning construction within pluralized public policing and the resulting cultural expressions risks embedding practice and conditions in the field that could ultimately be detrimental to the success of those relationships.

Bibliography

Armstrong, G. (1993) 'Like that Desmond Morris?' In D. Hobbs and T. May (eds) *Interpreting the Field: Accounts of Ethnography*. Oxford: Clarendon Press, pp. 3–44.

Association of Chief of Police Officers of England, Wales and Northern Ireland (2007) *Guidance on Police Community Support Officers*. London: ACPO.

Association of Chief of Police Officers of England, Wales and Northern Ireland (2011) *Restorative Justice Guidance and Minimum Standards*. London: ACPO.

Banton, M. (1964) *The Policeman in the Community*. London: Tavistock.

Barker, A. (2014) 'Communicating Security? Policing Urban Spaces and Control Signals.' *Urban Studies* 51(14): 3046–61.

Barrett, D. (2013) 'Put Bobbies Back on The Beat, Says Ex-Scotland Yard Chief.' *The Telegraph*, 23 November 2013. http://www.telegraph.co.uk/news/uknews/crime/10470439/Put-bobbies-back-on-the-beat-says-ex-Scotland- Yard-chief.html.

Bayerl, P.S., Karlović, R., Akhgar, B., and Markarian, G. (eds) (2017) *Community Policing—A European Perspective: Strategies, Best Practices and Guidelines*. Cham, Switzerland: Springer.

BBC (2006) '"Cheap" Support Policing Slammed.' *BBC News*, 18 January 2006. http://news.bbc.co.uk/1/hi/england/kent/4623960.

Birrell, S. J. (1978) *Sporting Encounters: An Examination of the Work of Erving Goffman and Its Application to Sport*. Unpublished PhD thesis, University of Massachusetts.

Bittner, E. (1967). 'The Police on Skid-Row: A Study of Peace Keeping.' *American Sociological Review* 32(5): 699–715.

Blagg, H., Pearson, G., Sampson, A., Smith, D., and Stubbs, P. (1988) 'Inter-Agency Co-operation: Rhetoric and Reality.' In T. Hope and M. Shaw (eds) *Communities and Crime Reduction*. London: HMSO, pp. 204–20.

Bott, E. (1957) *Family and Social Network*. London: Tavistock Publications.

Bourdieu, P. and Wacquant, L. J. D. (1992) *An Invitation to Reflexive Sociology*. Cambridge: Polity Press.

Branaman, A. (1997) 'Goffman's Social Theory.' In C. Lemert and A. Branaman (eds) *The Goffman Reader*. Oxford: Blackwell, pp. xlv–lxxxii.

Brogden, M., Jefferson, T., and Walklate, S. (1988) *Introducing Policework*. London: Unwin Hyman.

Brogden, M. and Nijhar, P. (2005) *Community Policing: National and International Models and Approaches*. Devon: Willan Publishing.

Brown, D. M. (2017) 'Beyond the Thin Blue Line? A Critical Analysis of Scotland's Community Wardens Scheme.' *Policing and Society* 27(1): 6–20.

Brown, J. and Heidensohn, F. (2000) *Gender and Policing: Comparative Perspectives*. London: Macmillan Press Ltd.

Brown, J., Maidment, A., and Bull, R. (1993) 'Appropriate Skill-Task Matching or Gender Bias in Deployment of Female Police Officers?' *Policing and Society* 3: 121–36.

Bryant, L., Dunkerley, D. and Kelland, G. (1985) 'One of the Boys?' *Policing* 1(4): 236–44.

Bryman, A. (2001) *Social Research Methods*. Oxford: Oxford University Press.

Bullock, K. and Leeney, D. (2014) On Matters of Balance: an Examination of the Deployment, Motivation and Management of the Special Constabulary.' *Policing and Society*. DOI: 10.1080/10439463.2014.949713.

Bullock, K. and Sindall, K. (2014) 'Examining the Nature and Extent of Public Participation in Neighbourhood Policing.' *Policing and Society: An International Journal of Research and Policy* 24(4): 385–404.

Cain, M. (1971) 'On the Beat: Interactions and Relations in Rural and Urban Police Forces.' In S. Cohen (ed.) *Images of Deviance*. Harmondsworth: Penguin, pp. 62–97.

Cain, M. (1973) *Society and the Policeman's Role*. London: Routledge.

Caless, B. (2007) 'Numties in Yellow Jackets: The Nature of Hostility Towards the Police Community Support Officer in Neighbourhood Policing Teams.' *Policing* 1(2): 187–95.

Chan, J. (1996) 'Changing Police Culture.' *British Journal of Criminology* 36(1): 109–34.

Chan, J. (1997) *Changing Police Culture: Policing in a Multicultural Society*. Cambridge: Cambridge University Press.

Chan, J. (2003) *Fair Cop: Leaning the Art of Policing*. With Chris Devery and Sally Doran. Toronto: University of Toronto Press.

Chan, J. (2007) 'Making Sense of Police Reforms.' *Theoretical Criminology* 11(3): 323–45.

Chao, G. T., O'Leary-Kelly, A. M., Wolf, S., Klein, H. J., and Gardner, P. D. (1994) 'Organizational Socialization: Its Content and Consequences.' *Journal of Applied Psychology* 79(5): 730–43.

Clary, E. G. and Snyder, M. (1999) 'The Motivations to Volunteer: Theoretical and Practical Considerations.' *Current Directions in Psychological Science* 8(5): 156–9.

Cockcroft, T. (2013) *Police Culture: Themes and Concepts*. London: Routledge.

College of Policing (2018) *Modernising Neighbourhood Policing Guidelines*. London: College of Policing. http://www.college.police.uk/What-we-do/Support/Guidelines/Neighbourhood-Policing/Pages/default.aspx.

Colover, S. and Quinton, P. (2018) *Neighbourhood Policing: Impact and Implementation. Summary Findings from a Rapid Evidence Assessment*. London: College of Policing. http://www.college.police.uk/What-we-do/Support/Guidelines/Neighbourhood-Policing/Documents/Neighbourhood_policing_impact_and_implementation.pdf.

Cooke, C. (2005) 'Issues Concerning Visibility and Reassurance Provided by the New "Policing Family."' *Journal of Community & Applied Social Psychology* 15: 229–40.

Cooper, C., Anscombe, J., Avenell, J., McLean, F., and Morris, J. (2006) *A National Evaluation of Community Support Officers*. Home Office Research Study 297. London: Home Office Research, Development and Statistics Directorate.

Cosgrove, F. (2011) *An Appreciative Ethnography of PCSOs in a Northern City*. Doctoral thesis, Northumbria University.

Cosgrove, F. (2015) '"I Wannabe a Copper": The Engagement of Police Community Support Officers with the Dominant Police Occupational Culture.' *Criminology and Criminal Justice*. DOI: 10.1177/1748895815599580.

Cosgrove, F. and Ramshaw, P. (2013) 'It Is What You Do as well as the Way that You Do It: The Value and Deployment of PCSOs in Achieving Public Engagement.' *Policing and Society* DOI:10.1080/10439463.2013.802787.

Crank, J. P. (2004) *Understanding Police Culture*, 2nd ed. Abingdon, Oxon: Routledge.

Crawford, A. (1997) *The Local Governance of Crime: Appeals to Community and Partnerships*. Oxford: Oxford University Press.

Crawford, A. (2006) 'Networked Governance and the Post-Regulatory State? Steering, Rowing and Anchoring the Provision of Policing and Security.' *Theoretical Criminology* 10(4): 449–79.

Crawford, A. (2008) 'Plural Policing in the UK: Policing beyond the Police.' In T. Newburn (ed.) *Handbook of Policing: Second Edition*. Cullumpton: Willan, pp. 147–81.

Crawford, A., Lister, S., Blackburn, S., and Burnett, J. (2005) Plural Policing: The Mixed Economy of Visible Patrols in England and Wales. Bristol: The Policy Press.

Crow, I. and Semmens, N. (2008) *Researching Criminology*. Maidenhead, Berkshire: The Open University Press.

Devroe, E. (2017) 'Bringing Politics Back into the Study of Policing? A Case Study on the Policing of Social Disorder in Belgium.' *Policing and Society* 27(1): 82–103.

Edwards, A. (2002). 'Learning from Diversity: The Strategic Dilemmas of Community Based Crime Control.' In G. Hughes and A. Edwards (eds) *Crime Control and Community: The New Politics of Public Safety*. Cullompton: Willan Publishing, pp. 140–66.

Ericson R.V. (1982) *Reproducing Order: A Study of Police Patrol Work*. Toronto: University of Toronto Press.

Ericson, R. V. (1995) 'Promoting Security: The Division of Expert Knowledge in Policing.' In K. Miyazawa and S. Miyazawa (eds) *Crime Prevention in the Urban Community*. Deventer: Kluwer Law and Taxation Publishers, pp. 11–60.

Falzon, M.-A. (2009) Introduction. In M.-A. Falzon (ed.) *Multi-Sited Ethnography: Theory, Praxis and Locality in Contemporary Research*. Farnham: **Routledge**, pp.1–24.

Field, J. (2008) *Social Capital*, 2nd ed. London: Routledge.

Fielding, N. G. (1988) *Joining Forces: Police Training, Socialization, and Occupational Competence*. New York: Routledge.

Fielding, N. G. (2008) 'Ethnography.' In N. Gilbert (ed.) *Researching Social Life* (3rd ed). London: Sage, pp. 266–84.

Fielding, N. G. (1994) 'Cop Canteen Culture.' In T. Newburn and E. Stanko (eds) *Just Boys Doing Business? Men, Masculinities and Crime*. London: Routledge, pp. 46–63.

Fielding, N. (1995) *Community Policing*. Oxford: Clarendon.

Fielding, N. G. and Fielding, J. (1992) 'A Comparative Minority: Female Recruits to a British Constabulary Force.' *Policing and Society* 2: 205–18.

Fielding, N. and Innes, M. (2006) 'Reassurance Policing, Community Policing and Measuring Police Performance.' *Policing and Society* 16(2): 127–45.

Flanagan, R. (2008) *The Review of Policing: Final Report*. London: Home Office.

Foster, J. and Jones, C. (2010) '"Nice to do" and Essential: Improving Neighbourhood Policing in an English Police Force.' *Policing* 4(4): 395–402.

Fulkerson, G. M. and Thompson, G. H. (2008) 'The Evolution of a Contested Concept: A Meta-Analysis of Social Capital Definitions and Trends (1988–2006).' *Sociological Inquiry* 78(4): 536–57.

Fyfe, N. (1991) 'The Police, Space and Society: The Geography of Policing.' *Progress in Human Geography* 15: 249–67.

Gill, M. (2015) 'Senior Police Officers' Perspectives on Private Security: Sceptics, Pragmatists and Embracers.' *Policing and Society* 25(3): 276–93.

Gill, M. and Mawby, R. (1990) *A Special Constable: A Study of the Police Reserve*. Aldershot: Avebury.

Goffman, E. (1959) *The Presentation of Self in Everyday Life*. Garden City, NY: Doubleday.

Goffman, E. (1990) [1959]. *The Presentation of Self in Everyday Life*. London: Penguin.

Greig-Midlane, J. (2014) *Changing the Beat? The Impact of Austerity on the Neighbourhood Policing Workforce*. Cardiff: UPSI.

Hammersley, M. and Atkinson, P. (1995) *Ethnography: Principles in Practice*, 2nd ed. London: Routledge.

Hanson, D. (2010) 'More Bobbies on the Beat Do Help to Cut Crime.' Letter to *The Guardian*, 18 February 2010 www.guardian.co.uk/uk/2010/feb/18/police-numbers-crime-figures-uk.

Hargreaves, J. (2016) *Police Workforce, England and Wales, 30 September 2015*. London: Home Office. https://www.gov.uk/government/statistics/police-workforce-england-and-wales-30-september-2015.

Hauber, A., Hofstra, B. Toornvliet, L., and Zandbergen, A. (1996) 'Some New Forms of Functional Social Control in the Netherlands and Their Effects.' *British Journal of Criminology* 36(2): 199–219.

Hannerz, U. (2003) 'Being There ... and There ... and There! Reflections on Multisite Ethnographies.' *Ethnography* 4(2): 201–16.

Heidensohn, F. (2008) 'Gender and Policing.' In T. Newburn (ed.) *Handbook of Policing: Second Edition*. Cullumpton: Willan, pp. 642–66.

Herbert, S. (1997) *Policing Space: Territoriality and the Los Angeles Police Department*. Minneapolis: University of Minnesota Press.

Her Majesty's Inspectorate of Constabulary (2014) *Policing in Austerity: Meeting the Challenge*. London: HMIC.

Her Majesty's Inspectorate of Constabulary (2016) *PEEL: Police Effectiveness 2015*. London: HMIC.

Herrington, V. and Millie, A. (2006) 'Applying Reassurance Policing: Is It "Business as Usual"?' *Policing and Society* 16(2): 146–63.

Higgins, A. (2017) *Neighbourhood Policing: A Police Force Typology*. London: The Police Foundation. http://www.police-foundation.org.uk/2017/wp-content/uploads/2017/06/neighbourhood_policing_a_police__force_typology.pdf.

Higgins, A. (2018) *The Future of Neighbourhood Policing*. London: The Police Foundation. http://www.police-foundation.org.uk/2017/wp-content/uploads/2010/10/TPFJ6112-Neighbourhood-Policing-Report-WEB.pdf.

Hofstra, B. and Shapland, J. (1997) 'Who Is in Control?' *Policing & Society* 6(4): 265–81.

Holdaway, S. (1983) *Inside the British Police: A Force at Work*. Oxford: Blackwell Press.

Holdaway, S. and Barron, A. (1997) *Resigners? The Experience of Black and Asian Police Officers*. Basingstoke: Macmillan Press Ltd.

Holdaway, S. and O'Neill, M. (2004) 'The Development of Black Police Associations: Changing Articulations of Race within the Police.' *British Journal of Criminology* 44(6): 854–65.

Holdaway, S. and O'Neill, M. (2006) 'Institutional Racism after Macpherson: An Analysis of Police Views.' *Policing and Society* 16(4): 349–69.

Home Office. (1995) *Review of Police Core and Ancillary Tasks Final Report*. London: HMSO.

Home Office (2001) *Policing a New Century: A Blueprint for Reform*. London: HMSO.

Home Office (2004) *Building Communities, Beating Crime: A Better Police Service for the 21st Century*. London: Home Office.

Home Office (2005) *Neighbourhood Policing: Your Police; Your Community; Our Commitment*. London: Home Office.

Home Office (2010) *Police Service Strength England and Wales, 31 March 2010*. London: The Home Office. https://www.gov.uk/government/statistics/police-service-strength-england-and-wales-31-march-2010.

Home Office (2011) *A Survey of Employers Involved in the Community Safety Accreditation Scheme Completed October to December 2010*. London: Home Office. https://www.gov.uk/government/publications/survey-of-employers-involved-in-the-community-safety-accreditation-scheme-december-2010.

Home Office (2017) *Police Workforce England and Wales, 31 March 2017*. London: The Home Office. https://www.gov.uk/government/statistics/police-workforce-england-and-wales-31-march-2017.

Hughes, G. and Rowe, M. (2007) 'Neighbourhood Policing and Community Safety: Researching the Instabilities of the Local Governance of Crime, Disorder and Security in Contemporary UK.' *Criminology and Criminal Justice* 7(4): 317–46.

Hunt, J. (1990) 'The Logic of Sexism among the Police.' *Women and Criminal Justice* 1(2): 3–30.

Innes, M., Hayden, S., Lowe, T., MacKenzie, H., Roberts, C., and Twyman, L. (2004) *Signal Crimes and Reassurance Policing*. Guildford: University of Surrey.

Innes, M. (2005) 'Why 'Soft' Policing is Hard: On the Curious Development of Reassurance Policing, How It Became Neighbourhood Policing and What This Signifies About the Politics of Police Reform.' *Journal of Community & Applied Social Psychology* 15: 156–69.

Jacobsen, J. and Saville, E. (1999) 'Neighbourhood Warden Schemes: An Overview.' *Crime Reduction Research Series Paper 2, Policing and Reducing Crime Unit*. London: The Home Office.

Johnston, L. (2005) 'From "Community" to "Neighbourhood" Policing: Police Community Support Officers and the "Police Extended Family" in London.' *Journal of Community & Applied Social Psychology* 15: 241–54.

Johnston, L. (2006) 'Diversifying Police Recruitment? The Deployment of Police Community Support Officers in London.' *The Howard Journal* 45(4): 388–402.

Johnston, L. (2007) '"Keeping the Family Together": Police Community Support Officers and the "Police Extended Family" in London.' *Policing & Society* 17(2): 119–40.

Johnston, L. and Shearing, C. (2003) *Governing Security: Explorations in Policing and Justice*. London: Routledge.

Jones, T. and Newburn, T. (1998) *Private Security and Public Policing*. Oxford: Clarendon Press.

Loader, I and Mulcahy, M. (2003) *Policing and the Condition of England: Memory, Politics and Culture*. Oxford: Oxford University Press.

Loader, I. and Walker, N. (2001) 'Policing as a Public Good: Reconstituting the Connections between Policing and the State.' *Theoretical Criminology* 5(1): 9–35.

Loader, I. and Walker, N. (2006) 'Necessary Virtues: The Legitimate Place of the State in the Production of Security.' In J. Wood and B. Dupont, B. (eds) *Democracy, Society and the Governance of Security*. Cambridge: Cambridge University Press, pp. 165–95.

Loftus, B. (2009) *Police Culture in a Changing World*. Clarendon Studies in Criminology. Oxford: Oxford University Press.

Longstaff, A., Willer, J., Chapman, J., Czarnomski, S., and Graham, J. (2015) *Neighbourhood Policing: Past, Present and Future. A Review of the Literature*. May 2015. London: The Police Foundation.

Lowe, T. and Innes, M. (2012) 'Can We Speak in Confidence? Community Intelligence and Neighbourhood Policing v2.0.' *Policing and Society: An International Journal of Research and Policy* 22(3): 295–316.

Macpherson, W. (1999) *The Stephen Lawrence Inquiry*, Cm 4262, London: HMSO.

Maitlis, S. and Christianson, M. (2014) Sensemaking in Organizations: Taking Stock and Moving Forward. *The Academy of Management Annals* 8(1): 57–125.

Manning, P.K. (1970) 'Talking and Becoming: A View of Organizational Socialization.' In J. D. Douglas (ed.) *Understating Everyday Life: Towards the Reconstruction of Sociological Knowledge*. London: Routledge and Keegan Paul, pp. 239–56.

Manning, P. K. (1977) *Police Work: The Social Organization of Policing*. Cambridge, MA: MIT Press.

Manning, P. K. (1997) *Police Work: The Social Organization of Policing*, 2nd ed. Prospect Heights, IL: Waveland Press.

Marcus G. E. (1995) 'Ethnography in/of the World System: The Emergence of Multi-Sited Ethnography.' *Annual Review of Anthropology* 24: 95–117.

Marks, M. (2004) 'Researching Police Transformation: The Ethnographic Imperative.' *British Journal of Criminology* 44: 866–88.

Marks, M. (2005) *Transforming the Robocops: Changing Police in South Africa*. Scottsville: University of KwaZulu-Natal Press.

Martin, C. (1996) 'The Impact of Equal Opportunities Policies on the Day-To-Day Experiences of Women Police Constables.' *British Journal of Criminology* 36(4): 510–28.

Martin, S.E. (1980) *Breaking and Entering: Policewomen on Patrol*. Berkeley: University of California Press.

Martin, S. (1994) '"Outsider Within" the Station House: The Impact of Race and Gender on Black Women Police.' *Social Problems* 41(3): 383–400.

Mason, M. (2009) 'Findings from the Second Year of the National Neighbourhood Policing Programme Evaluation.' *Home Office Research Report 14*. London: Home Office.

Matthews, R., Easton, H., Briggs, D., and Pease, K. (2007) *Assessing the Use and Impact of Anti-Social Behaviour Orders*. Bristol: Policy Press.

Mawby, R. C. and Wright, A. (2008) 'The Police Organisation.' In T. Newburn (ed.) *Handbook of Policing: Second Edition*. Cullumpton: Willan, Chapter 10.

May, T. (2011) *Theresa May Speech in Full*. 4 October 2011. http://www.politics.co.uk/comment-analysis/2011/10/04/theresa-may-speech-in-full.

McCarthy, D. (2014) *'Soft' Policing: The Collaborative Control of Anti-Social Behaviour*. Basingstoke: Palgrave Macmillan.

McCarthy, D. and O'Neill, M. (2014) 'The Police and Partnership Working: Reflections on Recent Research.' *Policing: A Journal of Policy and Practice* 8(3): 243–53.

Merritt, J. (2009) 'Plural Models of Policing—Legislating for Police Powers, a Cautionary Note from England and Wales.' *Policing: An International Journal of Police Strategies & Management* 32(2): 377–94.

Merritt, J. (2010) 'W(h)ither the PCSO? Police Perceptions of the Police Community Support Officer's Role, Powers and Future Directions.' *Policing: An International Journal of Police Strategies & Management* 33(4): 731–49.

Merritt, J. and Dingwall, G. (2010) 'Does Plural Suit Rural? Reflections on Quasi-Policing in the Countryside.' *International Journal of Police Science and Management* 12(3): 388–400.

Millie, A. (2013) 'The Policing Task and the Expansion (and Contraction) of British Policing.' *Criminology & Criminal Justice* 13(2): 143–60.

Muir, W. K., Jr (1977) *Police: Streetcorner Politicians*. Chicago: University of Chicago Press.

Muir, H. (2010) 'Give Police Community Support Officers a Break.' *The Guardian*, 23 September 2010. http://www.theguardian.com/commentisfree/2010/sep/23/pcsos-and-antisocial-behaviour.

Myhill, A. and Quinton, P. (2010) 'Confidence, Neighbourhood Policing, and Contact: Drawing Together the Evidence.' *Policing* 4(3): 273–81.

O'Neill, M. (2005) *Policing Football: Social Interaction and Negotiated Disorder*. Houndmills: Palgrave Macmillan Publishers.

O'Neill, M (2010) 'The Police Response to Crime.' In S. G. Shoham, P. Knepper, and M. Kett (eds) *The International Handbook of Criminology*. Boca Raton: CRC Press, pp. 483–510.

O'Neill, M. (2014a) 'The Case for the Acceptable 'Other': The Impact of Partnerships, PCSOs and Neighbourhood Policing on Diversity in Policing.' *Policing: A Journal of Policy and Practice* 9(1): 77–88.

O'Neill, M. (2014b) 'Ripe for the Chop or the Public Face of Policing? PCSOs and Neighbourhood Policing in Austerity.' *Policing: A Journal of Policy and Practice*. First published online 11 June 2014. DOI:10.1093/police/pau018.

O'Neill, M. (2016) 'Revisiting the Classics: Janet Chan and the Legacy of "Changing Police Culture".' *Policing and Society: An International Journal of Research and Policy* 26(4): 475–80. DOI: 10.1080/10439463.2016.1165997.

O'Neill, M. Marks, M., and Singh, A. M. (eds) (2007) *Police Occupational Culture: New Debates and Directions*. Oxford: Elsevier Science.

O'Neill, M. and McCarthy, D. (2014) '(Re)Negotiating Police Culture through Partnership Working: Trust, Compromise and the 'New' Pragmatism.' *Criminology and Criminal Justice* 14(2): 143–59.

Osborne, S. P. and Strokosch, K. (2013) 'It Takes Two to Tango? Understanding the Co-Production of Public Services by Integrating the Services Management and Public Administration Perspectives.' *British Journal of Management* 24: S31–S47.

Paoline, E. W., III (2003) 'Taking Stock: Toward a Richer Understanding of Police Culture.' *Journal of Criminal Justice* 31: 199–214.

Paskell, C. (2007) '"Plastic Police" or "Community Support"? The Role of Police Community Support Officers within Low-Income Neighbourhoods.' *European Urban and Regional Studies* 14(4): 349–61.

Pearson, G., Blagg, H., Smith, D., Sampson, A., and Stubbs, P. (1992) 'Crime, Community and Conflict: The Multi-Agency Approach.' In D. Downes (ed.) *Unravelling Criminal Justice*. London: Macmillan, pp. 46–72.

Pratchett, L. (2004) 'Local Autonomy, Local Democracy and the "New Localism".' *Political Studies* 52(2): 358–75.

Punch, M. (1979) *Policing the Inner City*. London: Macmillan.

Ranasinghe, P. (2017) 'Rethinking the *Place* of Crime in Police Patrol: A Re-Reading of Classic Police Ethnographies.' *British Journal of Criminology* 57(4): 867–84.

Reiner, R. (1978) *The Blue-Coated Worker: A Sociological Study of Police Unionism*. Cambridge: Cambridge University Press.

Reiner, R. (2000) 'Police Research.' In R. D. King and E. Wincup (eds) *Doing Research on Crime and Justice*. Oxford: Oxford University Press, Chaper 12.

Reiner, R. (2010) *The Politics of the Police*, 4th ed. Oxford: Oxford University Press.

Reuss-Ianni, E. (1983) *Two Cultures of Policing: Street Cops and Management Cops*. New Brunswick, New Jersey: Transaction Books.

Rogers, C. (2017) *Plural Policing: Theory and Practice*. Bristol: Policy Press.

Rowe, M. (2004) *Policing, Race and Racism*. Cullompton, Devon: Willan.

Rowland, R. and Coupe, T. (2014) 'Patrol Officers and Public Reassurance: A Comparative Evaluation of Police Officers, PCSOs, ACSOs and Private Security Guards.' *Policing and Society: An International Journal of Research and Policy* 24(3): 265–84.

Sacks, H. (1972) 'Notes on Police Assessment of Moral Character.' In D. Sudnow (ed.) *Studies in Social Interaction*. New York: Free Press, pp. 280–93.

Sackmann, S. (1991) *Cultural Knowledge in Organizations*. Newbury Park, CA: Sage.

Scarman, G. (1982) *The Scarman Report: The Brixton Disorders 10-12 April 1981*. London: Pelican.

Sampson, A., Stubbs, P., Smith, D., Pearson, G., and Blagg, H. (1988) 'Crime, Localities and the Multi-Agency Approach.' *British Journal of Criminology* 28(4): 478–93.

Schein, E. H. (1990) 'Organizational Culture.' *American Psychologist* 45(2): 109–19.

Shearing, C. D. and Ericson, R. V. (1991) 'Culture as Figurative Action.' *British Journal of Sociology* 42: 481–506.

Shearing, C. and Stenning, P. (1983) 'Private Security – Implications for Social Control.' *Social Problems* 30(5): 493–506.

Shearing, C. and Wood, J. (2003) 'Governing Security for Common Goods.' *International Journal of the Sociology of Law* 31(3): 205–25.

Silvestri, M. (2003) 'Visions of the Future: The Role of Senior Policewomen as Agents of Change.' *International Journal of Police Science and Management* 1(2): 148–61.

Skolnick, J. (1994) *Justice Without Trial: Law Enforcement in Democratic Society*, 3rd ed. London: Wiley.

Skolnick, J. and Fyfe, J. (1993) *Above the Law: Police and the Excessive Use of Force*. New York: Free Press.

Sklansky, D. (2007). 'Seeing Blue: Police Reform, Occupational Culture and Cognitive Burn-In.' In M. O'Neill, M. Marks, and A.-M. Singh (eds) *Police Occupational Culture: New Debates and Directions*. Oxford: Elsevier Science, pp. 19–46.

Smith, G. (2013) 'The Dramaturgical Legacy of Erving Goffman.' In C. Edgley (ed.) *The Drama of Social Life: A Dramaturgical Handbook*. Farnham, UK: Ashgate, pp. 57–74.

Smith, D. J. and Gray J. (1985) *Police and People in London: The PSI Report*. Aldershot: Gower.

Social Exclusion Unit (2001) *A New Commitment to Neighbourhood Renewal: National Strategy Action Plan*. London: The Cabinet Office.

Souhami. A. (2014) 'Institutional Racism and Police Reform: An Empirical Critique.' *Policing and Society* 24(1): 1–21.

Stenning, P. (1989) 'Private Police and Public Police: Toward a Redefinition of the Police Role.' In D. J. Loree (ed.) *Future Issues in Policing: Symposium Proceedings*. Ottawa: Canadian Police College, n. pag.

Strudwick, K., Jameson, J., and Rowe, J. (2017) 'Developing Volunteers in Policing: Assessing the Potential Volunteer Police Community Police Officer.' *Policing: A Journal of Policy and Practice* pax056. https://doi.org/10.1093/police/pax056.

Terpstra, J. (2017) '"Not Just One Node among Many" – Plural Policing in a State-Dominated Context: The Case of Austria.' *Policing and Society* 27(1): 68–81.

Tilley, N. (2008) 'Modern Approaches to Policing: Community, Problem-Orientated and Intelligence-Led.' In T. Newburn (ed.) *Handbook of Policing*, 2nd ed. Devon: Willan Publishing, pp. 373–403.

Utley, T. (2010) 'More Bobbies on the Beat? Forgive Me for Being Silly but Isn't That Blindingly Obvious to Everyone Except Our Politicians.' *The Daily Mail*, 24 September 2010. http://www.dailymail.co.uk/debate/article-1314755/More-bobbies-beat-Isnt-blindingly-obvious-everyone.html.

van Hulst, M. (2013) 'Storytelling at the Police Station: The Canteen Culture Revisited.' *British Journal of Criminology* 53: 624–42.

van Hulst, M. (2017) 'Backstage Storytelling and Leadership.' *Policing: A Journal of Policy and Practice* 11(3): 356–68.

Van Maanen, J. (1973) 'Observations on the Making of Policemen.' *Human Organization* 32: 407–18.

Van Maanen, J. (1975) 'Police Socialization: A Longitudinal Examination of Job Attitudes in an Urban Police Department.' *Administrative Science Quarterly* 20(2): 207–22.

Van Maanen, J. (1978) 'Kinsmen in Repose: Occupational Perspectives of Patrolmen.' In P. K. Manning and J. Van Maanen (eds) *Policing: A View from the Street*. Santa Monica, CA: Goodyear, pp. 115–28.

van Steden, R. (2017) 'Municipal Law Enforcement Officers: Towards a New System of Local Policing in the Netherlands?' *Policing and Society* 27(1): 40–53.

Waddington, P. A. J. (1999) 'Police (Canteen) Sub-Culture: An Appreciation.' *British Journal of Criminology* 39(2), 287–309.

Wakefield, A. (2003) *Selling Security: The Private Policing of Public Space*. Cullompton: Willan.

Wakefield, A. (2006) *The Value of Foot Patrol: A Review of Research*. London: Police Foundation.

Weisburd, D., Groff, E. R., and Yang, S. M. (2012) *The Criminology of Place: Street Segments and Our Understanding of the Crime Problem*. New York: Oxford University Press.

Westmarland, L. (2001) 'Blowing the Whistle on Police Violence: Gender, Ethnography and Ethics.' *British Journal of Criminology* 41: 523–35.

Westley, W. A. (1970) *Violence and the Police: A Sociological Study of Law, Custom, and Morality*. Cambridge, MA: The MIT Press.

White, A. (2012) 'The New Political Economy of Private Security.' *Theoretical Criminology* 16(1): 85–101.

White, A. (2015) 'The Politics of Police "Privatization": A Multiple Streams Approach.' *Criminology & Criminal Justice* 15(3), 283–99.

Wood, J. and Shearing, C. (2007) *Imaging Security*. Devon: Willan Publishing.

Wood, J., Sorg, E., Groff, E., Ratcliffe, J., and Taylor, C. (2014) 'Cops as Treatment Providers: Realities and Ironies of Police Work in a Foot Patrol Experiment.' *Policing and Society: An International Journal of Research and Policy* 24(3): 362–79.

Wooff, A. and Skinns, L. (2017) 'The Role of Emotion, Space and Place in Police Custody in England: Towards a Geography of Police Custody.' *Punishment and Society*. First published on 11 August 2017. DOI: 10.1177/1462474517722176.

Young, M. (1991) *An Inside Job: Policing and Police Culture in Britain*. Oxford: Clarendon Press.

Zedner, L. (2009) *Security*. London: Routledge.

Index

The manufacturer's authorised representative in the EU for product safety is Oxford University Press España S.A. of el Parque Empresarial San Fernando de Henares, Avenida de Castilla, 2 – 28830 Madrid (www.oup.es/en or product.safety@oup.com). OUP España S.A. also acts as importer into Spain of products made by the manufacturer.

www.ingramcontent.com/pod-product-compliance
Ingram Content Group UK Ltd.
Pitfield, Milton Keynes, MK11 3LW, UK
UKHW021133160926
475595UK00020B/23
9780198803676